Mr and Mrs Job

Mr and Mrs Job

Ellen van Wolde

SCM PRESS LTD

Translated by John Bowden from the Dutch *Meneer en mevrouw Job. Job in gesprek met zijn vrouw, zijn vrienden en God*, published 1991 by Uitgeverij Ten Have b.v., Baarn.

© Uitgeverij Ten Have b.v., Baarn 1991

Translation © John Bowden 1997

0 334 02712 8

First published 1997 by
SCM Press Ltd
9–17 St Albans Place London N1 0NX

Typeset by Regent Typesetting, London
and printed in Great Britain by
Biddles Ltd, Guildford and King's Lynn

Contents

A Brief Outline of the Book of Job

Ask a Catholic whether he or she has ever heard of Job and you will probably be told, 'Oh yes, Job is that pious man who loses everything.' Ask a Protestant what he or she knows about Job and you will be told, 'Job, he's that rebellious man who clashes with God because he thinks that his suffering is unjust.' The connotation here is that to rebel against God is one of the worst things that you can do. How is it that people have such different views about Job? The book of Job itself seems to encourage them.

Job the pious

The story begins with a description of Job as the model of a pious and good man for whom everything in life goes well. He is rich, he has many children and possessions, and he is a good man. He is religious and wants to serve God in an unselfish way. The satan, talking with God in heaven, puts a question-mark against this disinterestedness. The satan says, 'Yes, it's easy for anyone to be pious and good if they have all that their heart desires. But just let me get my hands on him; then we shall see how pious he is.' 'OK,' says God, 'you do that.' And the satan makes lightning strike the house in which all Job's children are, and they perish. All his cattle are stolen. He has nothing left. But Job doesn't give up God. When the satan has another conversation with God in heaven, he says, 'That's the case with most people. They continue to believe as long as you don't attack their own persons.' And the satan afflicts Job with ulcers, sickness and misery. The sick Job sits on the rubbish dump outside the city, but no curse comes to his lips.

Job the rebel

After this prologue, which portrays Job as the pious man *par excellence*, we have the second part of the book. Here Job is described as the prototype of the rebel. He says, 'Why does all this have to happen to me? Why does it happen to me and not to others?' Friends who visit Job to comfort him grieve with him. But when Job goes on and on, they've had enough and start discussing with him. This dialogue between Job and his friends takes up almost the whole book and displays a particular dynamic. To begin with, the friends still sympathize with Job, and also take the suffering that has come upon Job on their own shoulders. Gradually the friends speak increasingly fiercely to Job. Instead of being supportive friends, they finally even become his accusers. They want to tell Job what the cause of his suffering is, because they really think that Job has only himself to blame for it. It is so obvious: if you're rich and everything is going well with you, everyone wants to be your friend and no one feels the need to comment on your behaviour. But when things don't go well, your friends and other people prove to be moralists.

Job reacts angrily to the rebukes of his friends. 'I haven't committed any sins in the past as a result of which I now have to suffer so much. Of course, I too have my faults, but not so many that I have to suffer like this. God has done this to me, or he is looking on with indifference while this is happening to me. Why do I have to suffer like this? I don't believe your solution, that someone for whom things go badly has caused this by his sins. Just look around you. Don't good people fare badly and bad people fare well? Is that justice? You don't answer my objections. I want to hear from God, let him make it clear to me.'

God's answer

Many people ask things from God. So does Job. But he gets an answer, and that doesn't happen to everyone. God replies to Job: 'Where were you when I established the earth? Do you know the plan of creation? Do you know how the stars are kept together? Does the rain have a father, and do you know him? Do you have any power over the animals? Can you put a bit through the nose of a crocodile and a halter round his neck, and will he then follow you? Do you have any power over the hippopotamus? Tell me, do you know all this so well?' God celebrates the greatness of creation, a creation which is so extensive that human beings belong only on the periphery of it. And does such a minuscule part of creation want to criticize God or take responsibility?

God shows that human categories of justice are inappropriate for judging him and the whole of creation. The friends have tried to reduce God to a moral bookkeeper: add up the good deeds and subtract the evil deeds, and that gives you a total. God is reduced to a pedantic moralist, a guardian of the principle 'one good turn deserves another'. God shows that he does not fit into human categories. He rejects the idea of reward or punishment, of providence and predestination, because these reduce his plan to something measurable by human standards. In answer to Job's complaint, God offers a view of the cosmos from a divine perspective and shows that human categories fall short of his plan for the cosmos.

Job's reaction

God's answer makes Job see the cosmos from the perspective of the wholly Other. It opens his eyes to a view 'from above', and so he also sees himself from this divine perspective. He recognizes his previous ignorance and resigns himself to the fact that he is simply dust and ashes. He no longer needs to know God's unfathomable nature. He is freed from the false expectations which are aroused by the old idea of retribution and reward and which have misled his friends.

God's reaction to Job's reaction

God then reacts again and says that Job has done well to ask questions, not to keep to the old idea of retribution and not to succumb to the trite language of faith. For the questions which Job asked were real questions about himself and his relation with God, put from the perspective of an existential suffering. The friends, says God, were wrong in what they said. When they visited Job they did not begin to think from Job's perspective but argued from a general theology, a theology of retribution. Job begins with the reality of life, his life. The friends argue in general terms, not from a particular perspective. Therefore the friends are wrong about God, because they have pinned God to the scheme of reward and punishment.

The epilogue: all's well that ends well

After all this profundity, the book concludes with a happy ending. All goes well with Job again, as in the prologue of the book. Indeed it goes even better, since first he had seven thousand sheep and three thousand camels, and now he has fourteen thousand sheep and six thousand camels. For some readers this epilogue is a disappointment. They had finally been put off that idea of reward and retribution and now Job is rewarded again for his goodness. What are we to make of this? Elie Wiesel rightly remarks that with these new children Job does not have his previous children back, and that the pain and sorrow over them remains. I think that that is not the only thing the epilogue is about. But its function can be clarified only at the end of this book.

The book of Job as a triptych

The book of Job can be described as a play in three acts. In the first act or prologue the protagonist and his fellow actors are briefly introduced to us. The second act, or the dialogue, shows us the main character wrestling and undergoing a psychological development. His thought about God and perception of God become increasingly profound, against a background provided by the three characters of the friends, who do not change their ideas and adopt a fixed, immovable position. In the third and last act things get quite stormy. This shows us a lively dialogue between God, who appears on the scene for the first time, and Job, who reacts briefly. The story of Job is dramatic in the sense that it is the unfolding of a character whose thought and belief keep growing and become visible. The curtain falls after we have been given a glimpse of the new glorious situation in which Job ultimately finds himself.

The book of Job can be described not only as a play but also as a painting in the form of a triptych. The prologue stands on the left panel of the triptych and portrays the pious man Job in his relation to God. The central panel displays an extended, Hieronymus-Bosch-type painting with a wealth of details of the long conversations between God and his friends: it shows God in the many images that people have made of him. Finally, the right-hand panel depicts God as he sees himself: a picture of God and the world from above. It suggests Salvador Dali's painting with Jesus on the cross, seen from above and floating above the world.

The book of Job is not about the three panels separately, but about their links with one another and how as a triptych they form a single whole. The reader, confronted with human images of God and with a picture of God himself, is challenged by this tryptych to create his or her own connection. If we are to be able to do that as readers we must go deeper into the separate parts of the book. A detached look at the triptych or a reading of the book of Job can then lead to a personal assimilation and synthesis.

Date and place

We do not know precisely when the book of Job was written, but a dating around the fifth or fourth century before the beginning of our era is most probable. The Near Eastern society of that time was shaped by the political great power Persia. Everyone felt that this power was stable and immovable, as is evident from the saying 'a law of the Medes and Persians'. A small protected community of believing Jews lived in Israel and was surrounded by a world in which other religions were stronger than it was. For already a century and a half the Jews had been accustomed to live in a society in which Persian language, culture, politics and economic power were dominant. To a great extent foreign rulers, merchants, soldiers and workers shaped society. And of course they influenced Jewish thought indirectly and set people thinking. Pious Jews asked how it could happen that believers and good people had to suffer, while things went well with people who did not bother about God. It is striking that they put these questions in the mouth of a non-Jew, Job, who lives in Uz, a place which at all events cannot have been in Israel. In this way they make it clear that the book of Job is not about typically Jewish questions, but about universal human questions.

So in its present form the book of Job may have been written in the Persian period. However, it had already existed much longer as a story handed down by word of mouth. Two centuries earlier the prophet Ezekiel already mentioned three people who were known from antiquity for their great faith, namely Noah, Job and Dan'el. None of the three are Jews; they are prototypes of pious men known for perseverance in their faith despite the misery that they experience. Our text, too, seems to present Job as a timeless and legendary believer, known from of old, and therefore the actual time and context of the composition of the biblical book of Job is less important. And since people in any age are confronted with questions about how they are to deal with one another and God in a world full of misery and suffering, the book of Job has remained topical ever since the time it was written.

The Prologue: Job 1–2

1.1 There was once a man in the land of Uz; Job was his name. This man was blameless and upright, he feared God and kept well away from evil. 2. Seven sons and three daughters were born to him. 3. He had seven thousand sheep, three thousand camels, five hundred yoke of oxen, and five hundred she-asses, and very many servants. This man was more prosperous than anyone in the East. 4. His sons used to hold a feast, each on his appointed day in his own house; they also invited their three sisters to eat and drink with them. 5. And when the feasts were over, Job summoned them and purified them. Then he rose early in the morning and offered burnt offerings, one for each of them, for Job thought, 'Perhaps my sons have sinned and said good-bye to God in their hearts.' Thus Job did continually.

6. One day the sons of God came to pay their respects to YHWH, and the satan also came with them. 7. YHWH said to the satan, 'Where have you been?' The satan answered YHWH and said, 'I have been wandering round the earth.' 8. YHWH said to the satan, 'Have you noticed my servant Job? There is no one like him on the earth, a blameless and upright man, who fears God and keeps well away from evil.' 9. The satan answered YHWH and said, 'Is Job's fear of God disinterested? 10. Haven't you put a hedge around him and his house and all that he has? Haven't you blessed the work of his hands, so that his possessions have increased greatly over the land? 11. But stretch out your hand and touch all that he has; then see if he doesn't say good-bye to your face.' 12 YHWH said to the satan, 'All right, everything that he has is in your hand; but do not lay your hand on Job himself.' So the satan departed from the presence of YHWH.

The theme of the prologue

A good deal of the Bible, from Deuteronomy up to and including Proverbs, reflects the traditional dogma that everyone is rewarded or punished in accordance with the moral quality of his or her actions. This view of 'retribution' can also be found in the first part of Job 1, since the man in the land of Uz is said to be both good and prosperous, pious and rich. As readers we get the feeling that it all goes together. There is a direct relationship between the man's piety and his prosperity, between his extreme wealth and his extreme piety.

Once Job on earth has been described in this way, the camera is turned towards heaven. The omniscient narrator shows us how God talks with one of his servants in heaven, the 'accuser' or the satan. The satan is a kind of head of the secret service who has to detect evil deeds on earth and report them to God. God speaks and says: 'Have you seen my servant Job? On earth there is no one like him, just and godfearing.' However, God does not mention Job's possessions or wealth. It is the satan as accuser who emphasizes these in his question: 'Is Job disinterested in fearing God? Haven't you given him a hand? Doesn't he believe in you because he is rich and is protected by you?' From this moment on, the dialogue between God and the satan appears in quite a different light, and the contrast between the two becomes evident. God thinks that Job is pious and also rich. The satan suggests that Job is rich and therefore pious. In contrast to God, the satan begins from the principle of 'retribution', or the principle of 'one good turn deserves another'. He argues that this is the basis for all human behaviour, and therefore also for Job's behaviour. Job is pious only because things are going well for him.

Challenged by the satan, God begins the experiment of investigating the principle of retribution. He wants to test whether people continue to believe when their prosperity is taken away from them. This is an important question for God. Do people fear God in a disinterested way, or only in order to become better off? Because God cannot test everyone, Job, as the prototype of the pious man, is subjected to testing. If he doesn't pass the test, how can others? So the experiment is not simply carried out for the sake of human beings, but also and above all for God's own sake. How can God look himself in the eye as creator if all his creatures, even the most pious, love him only for what they get out of him?

One might wrongly suppose that it is the satan who starts this conversation in heaven. That isn't the case. God is the one who begins it by asking the satan whether he has noticed the pious Job. God thus judges Job's behaviour and life to be pious. The satan fulfils the role or function of accuser and does so with much verve. As accuser he puts the most important question that can be asked. On what is piety or belief in God based, on self-interest or God's interest? And this question is best put to the person who has just been described as the model of piety, Job. God himself can hardly play the role of opponent; the satan can do it better. The satan brings out the question which seems to live deep in God himself. To show that this is a question which preoccupies God himself, the narrator sets this scene in heaven. There the discussion can be carried on most sharply.

The structure of the prologue

1.13 One day, when his sons and daughters were eating and drinking in their eldest brother's house, 14. a messenger came to Job and said, 'The oxen were ploughing and the asses grazing beside them. 15. Then the Sabeans fell upon them and took them and slew the servants with the sword. I alone have escaped to tell you.' 16. As he was still speaking another one came and said, 'A fire of God fell from heaven and burned up the sheep and the servants, and consumed them. I alone have escaped to tell you.' 17. As he was still speaking, another one came and said, 'A Chaldean formation of three companies made a raid on the camels and took them, and slew the servants with the sword. I alone have escaped to tell you.' 18. While he was still speaking, another one came and said, 'Your sons and daughters were eating and drinking wine in their eldest brother's house. 19. Suddenly a great storm came up from the desert and struck all four corners of the house. I alone have escaped to tell you.' 20. Then Job arose, and tore his garments, and shaved his head, and fell upon the ground, prostrated himself, and said, 21. 'Naked I came from my mother's womb and naked I shall return. YHWH has given and YHWH has taken away; blessed be the name of YHWH.' 22. In all this Job did not sin, nor did he attribute anything improper to God.

2.1 One day the sons of God came to YHWH to pay their respects to him. The satan came with them to pay his respects to YHWH. 2. YHWH said to the satan, 'Where have you been?' The satan answered YHWH and said, 'I have been wandering around on the earth.' 3. YHWH said to the satan, 'Have you noticed my servant Job? There is no one like him on earth, a blameless and upright man, who fears God and keeps well away from evil. He still persists in his piety; you have set me against him for no good reason, to destroy him.' 4. The satan answered YHWH and said, 'Skin for skin! All that a man has he will give in exchange for his life. 5. Only stretch out your hand now, and touch his bone and his flesh, then see whether he will say good-bye to your face.' 6. YHWH said to the satan, 'All right, he is in your power; only spare his life.' 7. The satan went away from the presence of YHWH and struck Job with loathsome ulcers from the sole of his foot to the crown of his head. 8. Job took a potsherd to scrape himself with, and sat in the ashes. His wife said to him, 'Are you still persisting in your piety? Bless God/Say good-bye to God and die.' 10. But he said to her, 'You speak like one of those foolish women! If we accept good from the deity, why should we not also accept evil?' In all this Job did not sin with his lips.

The prologue is made up of six scenes. The first two scenes, 1.1–5 and 1.6–12, present us with two pictures: a picture of the earth with Job as one of the most pious and prosperous people, and a picture of heaven with a conversation between God and the satan about the disinterestedness of faith and the experiment to investigate Job's faith. The following scene, 1.13–22, describes the blows that hit Job. His cattle are stolen, his servants are killed and all his children perish. Job is hit hard, but he is far from being defeated, since he continues to believe. In the fourth scene, 2.1–6, the picture changes again and shows a second discussion between God and the satan in heaven. This conversation leads to another testing of Job. He suffers even greater blows from the heavenly experiment, and this is described in the fifth scene, 2.7–10. But even then Job does not abandon God. In the sixth and last scene Job's friends are introduced. They come to Job to comfort him now that he finds himself in such miserable circumstances.

Job certainly begins to raise questions immediately after this prologue, questions which arise out of his own life. The nub of these questions is, what is to be made of God when evil hits good people? This problem is central in the later conversations between Job and his friends. When something goes wrong there is certainly a principle of retribution. There would be no problems if only bad people fared badly. The problem arises when good people fare badly. Suffering seems to be a problem of the just, not of the unjust.

The prologue confronts us with what the book of Job is about. The constant shift from an earthly to a heavenly perspective and then back from a heavenly to an earthly perspective indicates that the key problem of the book of Job is how the two perspectives are to be connected. On the one side are the questions of the suffering of good people, put from the perspective of life here and now, 'contingent' or chance existence. On the other side the questions are put from the perspective from above, the 'transcendent' perspective, envisaged as being from God's position. The first perspective is that of every human being, whether believer, atheist or agnostic. For him or her the key question is: how can people deal meaningfully with a life into which they are thrown by chance, a life which need not be as it is? In other words, how can people give meaning to a life in which one person is by chance born in the rich West and gets a life of prosperity without having deserved it, and another is born in the Third World and gets a life of suffering that is equally unmerited? Why does one family get all the sickness and misfortune, and another go happily and prosperously through life? Why is there no justice in this life, and why are uselessness and unhappiness not distributed in equal portions to everyone? How as a human being do you give meaning to this? What are you to make of all this injustice and meaninglessness?

The second perspective is that of believers. They ask themselves the following questions. Why has God made the world as it is? Why has God included so much misery and wickedness in a creation which according to Genesis 1 he called 'good' or sometimes even 'very good'? How does God deal with the world and with human beings? How must people believe in God while the world is overflowing with meaninglessness and suffering? And above all, what does this require of human behaviour? From God's perspective, human life is not chance but necessity, whereas for human beings life can seem fortuitous and not necessary. Are human beings in a position to argue from this divine perspective of necessity? In the heavenly scenes in the prologue of Job we are looking over God's shoulder at people on earth. However, we readers get only a fleeting glimpse of the view from God and heaven and the question of disinterested human faith that goes with it, since after the prologue we remain on earth for a long time. Confronted with every possible answer to this from the human side, answers which are represented by the friends, we see God's perspective again only in his speech to Job at the end of the book. On this basis the structure of the whole book of Job can be indicated very briefly. In the prologue the rapid succession of scenes on earth and in heaven raises the question of the relationship between the earthly and the divine, between the contingent and the transcendent. After that, the greater part of Job, the dialogues, is about how people give different answers to this question from the perspective of earth. Then in God's speech we are given the purely transcendent picture, rounded off with a dialogue between God and Job which forms one great plea to combine the two.

Ambiguity in the book of Job

Many readers of the book of Job are inclined to say that the book is about human suffering in the world. They concentrate exclusively on the questions and answers which are worked out in Job's dialogues with his friends. Other readers think that we should look only at God's speech from the storm. For them everything turns on what God says, and we must keep to that. In my view, the relationship between these two perspectives is central to the book of Job: we must take the questions raised by concrete daily existence seriously, yet not pass over the question of God, of that which transcends daily life.

Just as in the alternating heavenly and earthly scenes of the prologue, so too in other sub-divisions of the book of Job (and here we think immediately of the dialogues), alternating or simultaneous and indeed even contrasting views can occur. The ambiguity produced by the existence of different perspectives side by side could then be a more general characteristic of the book. Whether that is the case remains to be seen. But we certainly must not primarily be concerned to exclude or select particular views at the expense of others. After a prologue like this it seems to me to make more sense to reckon with a possible ambiguity in the text.

Job's piety

If anything now seems clear and obvious, it is Job's piety as described in the prologue. It seems as if we have to answer the question whether or not Job is pious with a confident 'Yes, he is pious'. But this answer is less obvious than it seems. Let's follow the text of the prologue.

From the very first verse the story shows us Job as an upright, righteous and god-fearing man who keeps far from evil. We could almost say that he is an angel on earth. The text goes on to describe the large number of children that Job has and describes his material possessions at even greater length. Job's wife is not mentioned, either as a member of his family or among his possessions. She is evidently of no importance to him. Verse 4 relates how Job's sons have feasts to which they also invite their sisters. Do these feasts indicate that these sons are high-spirited people or do they characterize them as gluttons? I think that the text leaves that open. This openness is created by the words 'each on his own appointed day'. That can mean that there is a feast somewhere every day, now at the home of one son, and now at the home of another. If one day it has been the last son's turn to host the feast, then the next day it is the turn of the first son. Another possibility is that these words indicate that the sons each have a fixed day in the month or in the year on which they give a feast. The third and last possibility is that Job's sons give feasts with some regularity and it is said only that each organizes them in turn, a fair distribution of tasks.

Whereas there is this obscurity, and it is not clear even to Job as an anxious father whether they are behaving well or badly, verse 5 suggests that he begins from the negative possibility. He offers sacrifices for the supposed errors of his children so that, if necessary, they will be sanctified or purified. Job's reasoning is conveyed to us by the narrator, who knows his motives: 'For,' thought Job, 'perhaps my sons have sinned and said good-bye to God in their heart.' Job does not do this just once but whenever his sons have held a number of feasts. Is this a sign of Job's goodness, or is he over-anxious? He wants to remedy in advance by means of sacrifices something that is not certainly wrong. He thus gives the impression of being a believer who thinks that he must not make any mistakes and has to be in control of everything; he implicitly knows precisely what is good and what is wrong, or what God approves or disapproves of. What previously seemed to be a clear indication of Job's piety looks on closer inspection to be somewhat ambiguous. It could also prove less positive for Job.

The next scene takes place in heaven. God praises Job, calls him his servant and praises his piety and fear of God, whereas the satan is less certain of this piety. God and the satan represent the two positions over Job's faith: God is pro-Job and the satan is anti-Job. The next scene on earth (1.13–22) is the sequel to the previous scene on earth. On the very day that his sons and daughters were eating and drinking wine in the home of the oldest son, misery begins for Job. However, the ambiguity in the feasts mentioned earlier is not clarified. It remains unclear whether these feasts of the sons have a positive connotation like 'What a close family they are!' or a negative connotation like 'They were having yet another feast, those boozers'.

Now blow after blow strikes Job. We are told three times about these blows, in verses 16, 17 and 18, each time in the same words. The formula 'hardly had one messenger finished speaking that the next entered' gives the reader an impression of the great speed with which the blows follow one another. The tidings of disaster also get worse each time. first Job's cattle and asses are stolen and the servants looking after them are killed; then the sheep and the servants are struck by lightning; then the camels and their guards are stolen and killed; and finally to cap it all, a stormwind arises which kills all Job's children at the same time. The alternation of messengers is interrupted to some degree only by verse 18b. Here for the third time we are told that Job's sons and daughters were having a feast in the house of one of them. But immediately afterwards it becomes clear that mention of this feast of Job's children is technically necessary in order to explain how it is possible for them all to perish at the same time.

Job's reaction is striking. He tears his clothing to pieces, shaves his head bald and falls prostrate on the earth. But however sad he is, it is nowhere said that above all he mourns for his children. Everything happens to him on the same day, and so he grieves over everything at the same time, with no distinction being made between possessions and children. Even during the long discussions between Job and his friends Job never mentions his children. While they were still alive the children were mentioned only in connection with their feasts, and then above all apparently to emphasize Job's (scrupulous) piety. When they are dead they form an unexpressed part of Job's whole disaster. Job's children depend on Job, not only in the presentation of their life but also in their painful death. All the focus is on Job himself: both the narrator and Job himself think wholly from Job's perspective.

In his pious reaction to all this, Job too argues from himself and puts himself, and not for example his wife, at the centre of all his sorrow when he says,

'Naked I came from my mother's womb
and naked I shall return.'

The following Jewish story is told in connection with this verse.

The fox in the vineyard

Once a fox discovered a vineyard which was hedged in on every side. Suddenly he saw an opening and wanted to get in through it. But the opening was too narrow. He couldn't get through. What did he do? He fasted three days until he had become so thin that he could get into the vineyard through the narrow opening. He ate the succulent, ripe and tasty grapes until he was full and had got fat again. Then he tried to get out again through the opening, but this time too he failed. He had put on too much fat. So he fasted again for three days until he had become thin enough to get through the opening, as thin as he was when he had come in. When he stood outside he turned to the vineyard and said, 'Vineyard, vineyard, how fine and good you are, and how splendid and tasty are your fruits. But you are no use, because people leave you as hungry as they entered you.' So it is on this earth with its earthly struggle. Human beings come naked into this world and naked they must leave it again.

By this remark about the nakedness of existence Job shows that he accepts the misery that has befallen him. And despite his great sorrow he even adds two sentences of praise (1.21):

> 'Naked I came from my mother's womb
> and naked I shall return.
> YHWH has given and YHWH has taken away.
> Blessed be the name of YHWH .'

Isn't this statement, made at the moment when Job loses every-thing, the height of faith? Or does honesty require us to say that the text is ambiguous and open to two possible interpretations? The first possibility is to say that this is a true faith, the recogni-tion of YHWH as creator and thus as the one who gives the beginning and the end. I think that most readers read it like this, certainly in the first instance. Moreover we know the sentence 'the Lord has given and the Lord has taken away' as a saying used in death notices, and there we see it as an expression of faith. In Israel, too, this saying was a stereotyped expression for faith in times of misfortune. Job is suddenly overwhelmed with great misery and then uses this already existing and well-known formula of faith.

Another interpretation is that Job is described here as a prototype of the pious person. He speaks in the standard formula of faith, but hasn't yet worked through his own suffer-ing or experienced it in terms of his own individual situation. A true story can clarify these two interpretations.

In a family consisting of father, mother and three children, who are all firm believers and go to church, the second child, a small boy, is very fond of singing psalms and often speaks of his long-ing to see Jesus. Suddenly, one day the boy is run over by a car while playing and dies from his injuries. His parents grieve deeply, but they can cope with it. Their faith leads them to write in the notice of his death, 'the Lord has given and the Lord has taken away', and that is how they experience it. To each other and to friends they say, 'He always wanted so much to be with Jesus; who knows, maybe it's a good thing.' A year goes by in sorrow, but also with some tranquillity. After that year the mood changes. The mother in particular rebels and cannot cope with seeing all her son's friends growing up while her son is no more. They move house, because they cannot live any longer in the old house in which everything reminds them of him, while the other children are playing outside. The people around her are shocked and amazed. 'How could that happen? They had coped with it so well and their faith had supported them.' When she persists in her behaviour even after the move, in the course of time they begin to find her unreasonable. After all, they say, life goes on and she has two other children. Surely they can't be brought up only with misery? Even her husband can no longer go along with her and begins to become alienated from her. What has become of the reasonable woman he married and with whom he bore all the suffering? Gradually she also loses her faith. She cannot swallow the fact that a loving God, a powerful and just God, could have caused her this suffering. 'It was a fraud, a sedative from the church, to saddle me with such a picture of God,' she says, and she drops God. To the present day she goes on living in a godless world, embittered and disappointed, more preoccupied with her dead son than with the living, who do not understand.

Was this woman a believer before the death of her son or not? And when she put the death notice in the paper? Why not? But perhaps her faith was not yet fully developed and based too much on tradition and not enough on her own experience.

Perhaps the Job of the prologue is a pious and believing man whose faith had not been tested and has not grown fully. We can see a certain ambiguity in Job's piety. On the one hand Job is called a pious man by the narrator and by God, and is praised as such, and he behaves according to the standards of a believer. On the other hand Job is a believer who passively lets everything happen to him. The word 'fall' (*napal*), which appears several times in the prologue, is indicative here. Many blows befall Job. The Sabaeans fall upon his cattle (*napal* in 1.15), God's fire falls from heaven (*napal* in 1.16), a storm wind falls on the house where the children are (*napal* in 1.19). How does Job react to all this? He shaves the hair of his head and falls to the earth (*napal* in 1.20), praying, 'the Lord has given and the

Lord has taken away, blessed be his name.' Job remains passive and accepts everything that happens to him, expressing this in a traditional creed. Only later will he raise himself and his voice and oppose God. It is precisely at the moment when he begins to fight with God that Job becomes a more active believer instead of a passive and pious man, a believer who wants to look both God and the reality of his own life in the eye. So I would want to opt for a degree of ambiguity over Job's piety in the prologue. Both options are there in the prologue and possibly both are being worked out in the rest of the book.

Job's wife

The prologue describes Job as a believing man in terms which correspond to those used to describe Noah, another legendary pious man in history. The wives of these men, Noah and Job, also resemble each other to some degree. To make that clear here is a fictitious letter from Noah's wife and Job's wife.

Dear readers,

Allow us to introduce ourselves. We are the wife of Job and the wife of Noah. We don't have names of our own. We do appear in the Bible, but only anonymously and as spouses. First something about our background.

I appear as a character in the flood story in Genesis. I'm not so important. My sons are more important than I am. And my husband is even more important. He is the famous Noah, the hero of the flood. Look it up in your Bible; I'm there, but I'm always named after Noah and my sons. I can't complain; my daughters-in-law come off even worse than I do. They are only mentioned as a trio. Anonymous and just a member of the extended family, that's bad enough. Sometimes I think that I was too compliant and that I should have raised my voice, so that the author of the story would also have given my opinion. But my husband Noah isn't much of a talker either. He's a silent man, but a good one. I'm glad to be able to serve him. What makes me cross is that the only person who has given me a voice, the composer Benjamin Britten in Noye's Fludde, *has made me a carping fishwife. I grant that at that time there were* lots of fish with all that water, but surely that doesn't make me a fishwife? And he even makes my dear husband hit me. Whereas he was the very personification of tolerance. I haven't been brought up to come into the foreground. So I've teamed up with Job's wife. Together we've seized this opportunity to make our voice heard, two of the countless anonymous figures of history. I didn't do it by myself. She's more capable; she's also got rid of the stylistic mistakes in this letter and corrected everything. I'm glad to let her take over.

Do you know the book of Job and have you read what is said about me at the beginning of the book? It describes how Job, my husband, was first rich and after that lost everything. He's lost absolutely everyone and everything and is alone in the world. Later, however, it proves that I'm still alive, but apparently I don't count. The fact that I'm still mentioned by the narrator is simply for me to play the role of the satan on earth. Perhaps I would have done better to die and not go down in history as that bad wife of Job, who clearly wants to put him on the wrong track. Abel Herzberg has described it well in his book Three Red Roses. The main character, who is very like my husband (or in these modern times should I speak of my 'ex-?'), says, 'Your marriage, Job, wasn't very good, rather like mine. You didn't treat your wife very well or portray her very well; you gave her a role which would put you in a good light so that you came out of it well.' I call this yet another psychological insight. It's better than Britten, who has attributed some of my assertive characteristics to Noah's wife, and the poor woman is completely destroyed by them. She's the personification of virtue and modesty. She has to be, to cope with marriage to such a righteous man as Noah. My husband has rather more spirit; he's also more of a rebel. The people around him, even his best friends, get wind of this. And he attacks even God. Noah doesn't. Noah listens and obeys and keeps quiet. Perhaps he speaks only through sacrifices.

But now, in a time when women dare to raise their voice, we too are taking up the pen and telling you all to give a clear and understandable voice to those who have no voice in history. We aren't speaking for ourselves alone, but in the name of all those who have disappeared in the Bible and in history, but who have

now come to life. Today we've been impudent enough to push
ourselves forward and even raise our voices. Noah's wife wants
to offer her apologies for this impudence, but I think it's our
right to get a hearing. We hope that other women will follow
our example.

With friendly greetings,
Noah's wife
Job's wife

You should be Job's wife! From the beginning of the prologue
onwards, the narrator has not found much room for her. Job is
described as a 'gentleman farmer', the father of many children,
the master of many servants, but his wife has not been mentioned, either in times of prosperity or in times of misfortune.
The description of Job in the prologue shows much similarity to
that of the patriarchs Abraham, Isaac and Jacob in Genesis, but
the wives of the patriarchs play a much greater role than Job's
wife. The wives of the patriarchs have names; they make an
appearance and the narrator tells many stories about them in
particular. The only time that Job's wife appears is in 2.9, and
the negative assessment of the narrator is abundantly clear.
Job's wife is described as one of those foolish women and even
seems to function as a representative of the satan on earth.

> His wife said to him,
> 'Are you persisting in your piety?
> Say good-bye to God/Bless God and die.' Job said to her,
> 'You speak like one of those foolish women!
> If we accept good from God,
> why should we not also accept evil?'

In the Hebrew text Job's wife has to make do with this short
sentence of her own and her husband's biting reply. But she gets
more attention in the later Jewish translations or commentaries
on the book of Job. In the Septuagint translation from the third
century BCE the prologue is translated literally from Hebrew
into Greek; only to the sentences about Job's wife are a number
of verses added. In translation they read as follows:

> After a long time his wife spoke to him:
> 'How long will you bear this and say,

"Behold, I will bear with it for a short time still
in expectation of the hope of my redemption."
Behold, your memory is swept from the earth,
your sons and daughters, the pains and difficulties of my
womb,
for whom I suffered and worked in vain.
You are sitting in the filth with the worms
and you bring the night into the open air.
And I go as a day labourer through the land
from place to place and from house to house;
I wait for the sun to go down
to find rest from the toil and the pain
which now overcome me.
Say a word against the Lord and die!'

A century later the Septuagint translation became the starting
point for a Jewish commentary on the book of Job which was
written in Greek and is called the Testament of Job. As the title
already indicates, this book is a testament or autobiography of
Job. In it Job relates his life story to his children and emphasizes
the prominent role that his wife has played in his life. He
devotes such a long part of the account of his life to her that it
occupies six chapters of the book, 21 to 26. Abbreviated and
freely translated these chapters tell the following story. Job
speaks to his children and says:

For forty-eight years I sat on the heap of ashes outside the city
because of my sickness and I saw with my own eyes my humble
wife carrying water to the house of a particularly cruel person
whose servant she had become, so that she could buy bread and
bring it to me . . . After eleven years they even stopped her
bringing bread to me, and she had only her own bread. She
received her bread and shared it with me and said with pain in
her heart, 'Woe is me, soon he will no longer be able to get
enough bread.' But she did not hesitate to go to the market
place to beg bread from those who sold it in order to bring it to
me so that I too could eat. The satan knew this and therefore
disguised himself as a breadseller. By chance it happened that
my wife went to him to ask for bread, because she thought that
he was a human being. And the satan said to her, 'Pay the price

and take what you want.' But she answered him, 'Where am I going to get the money from? Don't you know what disasters have overtaken us? If you have any feeling, show compassion, but if you do not, then . . . ' He answered her again, 'If you had not deserved these disasters, you would not have had them. Now, if you have no money, give me the hairs of your head as payment and take three loaves. Perhaps that will let you live three days longer.' She said to herself, 'What is my hair worth to me compared with my hungry husband?' She loosened her hair and said to him, 'Cut it off.' Then he took a pair of scissors and cut off the hairs of her head and gave her three loaves, while everyone looked on.

When she had received the loaves, she brought them to me. But the satan had followed her on her way to me and confused her heart. When my wife came to me, she burst into tears and said to me, 'Job, Job, how long will you keep sitting on this heap of ashes outside the city, thinking, "Yet still," because you hope for your redemption? I have become a servant and a vagrant who goes from place to place. For all your remembrance has disappeared from the earth, my sons and daughters, the pains and hurts of my womb, for whom I fought in vain, with pain and difficulty . . . Everyone says in amazement, "Is that Sitidos, Job's wife? The one who protected her room with fourteen curtains and had door after door, so that only those who were really thought worthy gained access to her? Now she is exchanging her hair for bread . . ." Job, Job, many words are said, but I say to you, "The weakness of my heart shatters my bones. Stand up, and when you have eaten the loaves, be satisfied. Say something against the Lord and die! Then I will be free from all the misery that comes through my toil for your body.'

I answered her, 'Behold, I have lived for seventeen years with my sickness, borne the worms in my body, and have never been so smitten as now, because you say, "Say something against the Lord and die." I am suffering just as much from all our miseries as you are, from the destruction of our children and our possessions. Do you want to have it on your conscience that through our talk against the Lord we are being alienated from our great treasure? And why do you no longer remember the great many good things with which we used to live? If we accept the good things from the hands of the Lord, must we not also bear the bad things? Let us be patient in everything until the Lord feels for us and has compassion. Don't you see the devil standing behind you? Don't you realize that he is confusing us in order to mislead me as well? For he is trying to exploit you as one of the unfeeling women who undermine the integrity of their husbands.'

In this later Jewish elaboration of the biblical text, Job's wife comes off much better than in the basic Hebrew text. Now people notice her and the misery that has overtaken her. She speaks the same words as in the Hebrew text, but the more extended context in the Septuagint and in the Testament of Job makes her concern for her husband and her despair more clearly visible. These make her urge her husband to put his head on her lap. The recognition of her suffering and toil gives the reader a more positive picture of Job's wife, and the meaning of what she says to her husband is easier to understand.

Precisely what does Job's wife say?

We must go back to the Hebrew text of the biblical book of Job to see precisely what Job's wife says there in 2.9:

'His wife said to him,
"Are you persisting in your piety?
Bless God/ say good-bye to God and die."'

The first part of what Mrs Job says (9a) is a literal repetition of what God himself said earlier in 2.3: 'Job still persisted in his piety.' The second part of what she says seems to agree with what the satan says in 1.11 and 2.5b, 'See if he will not say good-bye to your face.' Job's wife is thus repeating God and the satan and adding a new element, namely 'Die'.

The ambiguity of the book of Job indicated above is also there in what Job's wife says. She not only uses elements of statements by God and the satan, but she also uses the word *barak* in an ambiguous way. Normally *barak* means 'bless'. In the prologue of Job it occurs with this meaning twice, namely in 1.10, when the satan says that YHWH has always blessed and protected Job, and in 1.21, when Job says that the name of YHWH is blessed. But three times, in 1.5, 11 and 2.5, *barak* has the opposite meaning, namely to 'curse' God or, to use the word-play in the Hebrew, 'say good-bye' (adieu) to God. Job is afraid that his sons have said good-bye to God in their hearts, while the satan has the firm conviction that after all the misery Job will say good-bye to YHWH.

In what sense does Mrs Job now use this word *barak*? The first possibility is that she advises her husband to curse or say good-bye to God. This automatically entails the consequence that in reaction to this cursing God will abandon Job himself and that Job will die. This interpretation is based on the meaning of *barak* as curse, to be found in 1.5, 11 and 2.5. The second possibility is that she tells her man that he must bless God and die with this blessing on his lips, possibly by killing himself. *Barak* then means bless, as in 1.10 and 1.21. Given Job's reaction to his wife's words, both interpretations remain possible. Job refuses to take up his wife's challenge. In so doing, on the one hand he can be indicating that he does not want to curse God and thus that he will not abandon God, no matter what. On the other hand he can be indicating that he does not want to bless God, far less kill himself.

What Mrs Job says is thus ambiguous and open to two interpretations. It is characteristic that in the history of the reception of the book of Job, Job's wife is regarded almost exclusively as a voice of the satan on earth. Then only the second part of her remark is noted and *barak* is understood solely in the sense of cursing. That is to overlook the fact that in the first part of her remark she is saying what God himself had said earlier. I think that we must do justice to the ambiguity of 2.9 and allow both elements, the element in what Job's wife says which corresponds to God and the element which corresponds to the satan, along with the double meaning of *barak*, to stand.

What is the precise effect of what Mrs Job says to her husband? We can discover that only if we compare what Job says in reaction to his first series of blows before his wife had spoken with what he says in reaction to the second series of blows after his wife has spoken. Job reacts before and after his wife has spoken as follows:

1.21–22	2.10
YHWH has given and YHWH has taken away.	If we accept good from the deity why should we not then accept evil?
Blessed be the name of YHWH.	
In all this Job did not sin.	In all this Job did not sin with his lips.

The number and character of the differences in what Job says is striking. The first time that he speaks, Job calls God by his name YHWH. He recognizes him and addresses him as Lord. The second time, immediately after the remark by his wife, Job talks about God as 'the deity' *(ha-elohim)*. That sounds more distant by comparison with the earlier use of the name YHWH. Moreover he does not speak *to* God but *about* God, not to YHWH but about the deity. The second difference is closely connected with this. In 1.21 God explicitly praises and blesses Job; in 2.10 there is no longer mention of a blessing. Job continues to recognize that human beings receive everything from God, but for the first time mentions not only the good but also the evil that comes from God. However, all this does not mean that Job now begins to curse, since we are explicitly told, 'Job did not sin.' In the end Job does not bless or curse in 2.10. So in any case his wife does not get her way, whether we understand her remark as an incitement to cursing or as an incitement to blessing. A third difference is that the first time Job makes a statement and the last time he asks a question. His certainty seems to have been replaced by uncertainty. A fourth difference indicates something similar. In 2.10 we read that Job 'did not sin with his lips', whereas in 1.21 we had 'Job did not sin'. He can get no blessing or sin through his lips, but inside some doubt seems to have been sown. Because the words used are precisely the same, the difference 'with his lips' is striking. But the fifth and last difference in what Job says before and after his wife's words is the most striking. The perspective from which Job speaks has totally changed. In 1.21 he is speaking from a heavenly or divine perspective: 'YHWH gives and takes'. By contrast, in 2.10

he is speaking from an earthly or human perspective: 'If we receive good, why should we not also receive evil?'

The literary function of Job's wife in this story is intriguing. On the one hand she is completely overshadowed by her husband and seems irrelevant to the course of the narrative. On the other hand she makes Job reflect by what she says, although he has already rejected her words as foolish. But her speaking has an effect. Because Job is confronted for the first time with his own death, and is offered the choice of *barak* blessing or *barak* cursing, he is compelled to react. And the one who had previously opted for blessing and not sinning, from now on leaves both behind. His wife introduces death into his own life and raises doubts in him. Job is no longer so certain about everything, and he begins to ask questions. He even begins to argue from an earthly perspective, and no longer takes the earlier perspective of YHWH for granted. As the story develops, Job's wife therefore plays an important role. Through her, Job can change from being a believer who knows for certain into a questioner. No book would probably have been devoted to a believer who was certain about everything, and if it had been, it would certainly not be an exciting book. The book of Job has only become lifelike and authentic as a result of the doubt, the combativeness and the disputatiousness of someone who wants to confront his belief in God with his life and death, his suffering and misery.

All this shows that the first chapters of the book of Job form a real prologue: they create the conditions under which the story can begin to develop. In the first part of the prologue we read a description of Job as a man of exemplary piety. He is portrayed as a perfect believer who sees his life from God's perspective and identifies his perspective with that of God. He tries to imagine what is good and bad in God's sight and wants also to see his children in that light. Whether he also thinks of or for his wife in this way is not clear; at any rate, the narrator does not say anything about it. Even after the first blows Job continues to argue from the divine perspective. Only after the second series of blows, which are mentioned in the text only after and therefore also as a result of what his wife says, does Job for the first time speak from the perspective of a human being and not from that of God. Only through this change of perspective, and thus from that moment on, can the confrontation of the perspectives of human beings and God become the main theme of the book of Job. This confrontation could not have begun had not Job undergone a change, which also happens as a result of what his wife says.

The heavenly perspective; a question of chinam

The alternation of heavenly and earthly perspectives in the prologue is also evident in our exposition of the prologue. We began with the heavenly conflict, and after that we spent a long time on earth with Mr and Mrs Job. Now, in analogy to the alternation in the prologue itself, we return to higher spheres, to God and his official, the satan.

In the first heavenly scene (1.6–12), God and the accuser discuss how upright and pious Job is. The satan puts the key question in this connection in 1.9:

'Does Job fear God for nothing (*chinam*)?'

The word *chinam* has a double meaning, namely 'without cause' or 'without purpose', or 'for no reason' or 'for nothing'. In fact *chinam* indicates that something is not based on causality. There is neither a cause or reason nor a consequence or aim behind something that is *chinam*. In the first heavenly scene *chinam* functions with the meaning of 'without purpose', when the satan asks whether Job is pious with the aim of becoming rich. God and the satan decide on an experiment, with Job as the ideal test-case. They want to investigate whether there is a relation between faith and prosperity, and thus whether there is a faith without a view to gain. Now the experiment has been carried out, and Job seems still to be pious. What does that prove in terms of the experiment? It can mean that piety is not the result of prosperity, in other words that faith without a view to gain is possible. The test has then proved successful. But it can also mean that the experiment has not been carried out properly. If health is also included in prosperity, the mistake is not to have tested whether Job remains pious when he becomes sick. The test has to be continued. This

latter is evidently the case, since in the second heavenly scene
YHWH and the satan resolve to continue the experiment. Before
deciding to extend the test, YHWH says:

'Job still persists in his piety;
you have set me against him
to destroy him for no good reason (*chinam*)' (2.3).

God recognizes that Job has been tested without reason
(*chinam*) in the framework of the experiment. In contrast to the
first heavenly scene in which *chinam* meant 'without purpose',
here YHWH uses *chinam* in the sense of 'without cause'. The
experiment itself is not *chinam*, since it has a reason and a purpose, namely an investigation of the possibility of disinterested
faith. However, the choice of Job as a test-case is *chinam*, as
God himself explicitly recognizes: 'I have destroyed Job without
reason.' Can it be clearer? God is simply saying that the suffering of Job is not the result of his pious behaviour. So God
recognizes that it is possible for righteous people to suffer. Thus
this statement by God gives the proof that God does not act in
accordance with the principle of retribution. We may feel from
our human perspective that this is very unjust, and think it dis-
honest of God not to keep to our human categories of justice.
However, the narrator allows us to look from the divine perspective. The principle of retribution is not an element in God's
investigation into disinterested human faith. Even after YHWH
has recognized that he has ruined Job without reason, he gives
the satan permission to smite Job again (2.6). So he is not
ashamed of his action towards Job.

Through the two scenes in heaven the narrator presents the
collapse of the principle of retribution from the divine perspective. In the later dialogues the narrator will present everything
from the perspective of Job and his friends. Here they will
always raise the question of retribution, the principle of justice
that they do not encounter often enough in the world. Job will
then keep saying that this justice does not exist. The friends will
repeat that there is retribution, but that we, weak human
beings, do not see it. Right at the end of the book God (in 42.7)
will react and say, 'You, Job have spoken rightly and not your
friends. Justice or what human beings call justice is not present

in the creation in the way people would like.' The prologue has already moved ahead of this. The heavenly scenes, and especially the double use of the term *chinam*, show that what is necessary before God is a faith for no reason (*chinam*), whereas for human beings this is not a necessity but a possible choice. At the same time it becomes clear that what is a necessity for human beings, namely justice by human standards, is not a necessity for God but *chinam* or a free choice. We can only conclude that the differences between the divine and the human perspective are enormous. But Job as yet has no knowledge of all this; the narrator has simply granted the readers a brief look into heaven. Job is sitting on earth and has no grasp of it. In a passionate discussion with his friends, he tries to get more insight into it all.

The introduction of Job's friends

At the end of the prologue three of Job's friends appear on the scene. They have heard that things are going badly for Job and they come from afar and from different directions. Their names are Eliphaz, Bildad and Zophar. The following Jewish midrash relates their meeting.

Withered leaves

Job had three friends who were particularly fond of one another and who had above all taken to Job. Each of them had planted three trees in his garden and carved the names of his friends on them. They watched over their trees and looked after them lovingly and carefully. These fresh and blooming trees attracted the attention of everyone who went by. They were a divine sight for everyone who saw them. All their visitors delighted in them. One day the three friends went into their gardens and saw to their dismay that the tree on which the name of Job was written had withered and that its leaves were dry and hard. They were very surprised at this. Each thought to himself, 'Something serious has happened to Job. I shall go to see him and help him in his need.' Then Job's three friends hastened, left their houses and their land, and went to Job. When they arrived at the gate

*of the city they recognized one another and one of them asked
another, 'Why have you left your house and your land and
come here?' He replied, 'The tree on which Job's name was
carved suddenly withered, and I have come here to see how he is
faring.' Then Job's two other friends said, 'What happened to
your tree also happened to our trees, and we too have come to
support him in need.' While they were talking together, they
entered the city and found Job. They saw that he had sores all
over his body and was suffering much pain. Then they lifted up
their voices and wept. They tore their garments and sat on the
ground.*

Job's friends come to him and are shocked at what they see.
Is this their friend of whom they are so fond? They expected a
prosperous man in an attractive house, but now they see a filthy
and scabby old man on a heap of ashes. Ulcers cover his body
and he sits there scratching them with a potsherd. The reader
knows what they do not know, namely that the satan or accuser
had already forecast all this: layer by layer he will strip off Job's
skin. The satan does his job well. Eczema and ulcers attack Job's
body; bit by bit his skin flakes off and scratching does not help.

The friends are so concerned about Job that they go to him
and sit silently around him, sharing in his sorrow. What more
can you do in such a situation? Words fall short in suffering,
real suffering, with someone who is in pain and has just lost all
his children. Any talk disguises the unfathomable depth of the
sorrow. They prove good friends, really involved and concerned. They don't come with wise counsel or encouraging
advice. They don't say, 'Rise above it.' No, they sympathize.
They sit there for seven days and seven nights. This is sufficient
indication and introduction of them as real friends.

Then Job opens his mouth and we hear a long and heartfelt
cry, apparently not addressed to anyone in particular. He bears
witness to his pain to God and the world, to himself and his
friends, to anyone who will listen. This monologue by Job forms
as it were the opening area of a long piece of music with succes-
sive duets between Job and his friends, in which one sings a tone
higher and the other a tone lower. These duets are arranged in
cycles and are concluded by a second long aria by Job. So it all

looks like this (the numbers refer to the relevant chapters in the book of Job):

Job's monologue   3

First round of conversations   4–14
Eliphaz–Job
Bildad–Job
Zophar–Job

Second round of conversations 15–21
Eliphaz–Job
Bildad–Job
Zophar–Job

Third round of conversations 22–27
Eliphaz–Job
Bildad–Job

Job's monologue 28–31.

Job's Monologue: Job 3

1. After this Job broke silence and cursed on his day.
2. Job said,
3. 'Away with the day on which I was born,
   and with the night on which it was announced,
   "A boy has been conceived."
4. May that day remain darkness;
   may God on high not ask after it;
   may no light shine upon it.
5. May darkness and the shadow of death claim it;
   may a covering of clouds lie over it;
   may a darkening of the sun deter it.
6. May darkness take away that night;
   may it not be counted among the days of the year;
   may it not be admitted to the cycle of the months.
7. May that night remain barren;
   may no joyful cry be heard in it.
8. May those who curse the day damn it;
   those who have the skill to rouse Leviathan.
9. May the stars of its dawn remain dark;
   may they hope in vain for light;
   may they not see the glinting of the morning.
10. It did not lock the doors of my mother's womb,
    nor did it hide trouble from my eyes.
11. Why did I not die at birth?
    Why did I not choke when I left the womb?
12. Why were there knees to receive me?
    Or breasts to suckle me?
13. Then I would now be lying down, be at rest,
    sleeping, undisturbed,
14. next to kings and princes of this world,
    who built ruins for themselves,
15. or next to rulers who had gold,
    and filled their houses with silver.
16. If only I had been put in the ground as an abortion,

as a baby who never saw the light.

17. There the evildoers cease from their pursuits;
    there those whose strength is exhausted rest.
18. There prisoners are at ease together,
    they do not hear the voice of the taskmaster.
19. The small and the great are there alike
    and the slave is free from his master.
20. Why does He give light to the suffering
    and life to the embittered people?
21. They long for death, but it will not come;
    they look out for it more than for treasure.
22. They should be exceeding glad,
    rejoice, because they have found the grave.
23. (Why give life) to a human being whose way is hidden;
    now that God has hedged him around?
24. My sighing serves as my daily bread,
    and my groanings are poured out like water.
25. For what I most feared has come upon me,
    and what I dreaded has befallen me.
26. I have no happiness, no rest,
    no peace, only ongoing unrest.'

Earlier I called Job's monologue in chapter 3 an opening aria. Perhaps the word aria gives the wrong idea, since what Job says is not an attractive song which is good to listen to. Job's cry, which is striking in its directness, cuts straight through our souls. But the style is purely poetic and the content is dramatic. And that makes it seem like an aria.

In the very first sentence the narrator sums up what Job is going to say. That prepares us to some degree for what is to come. This summary says in unmistakable terms: 'After this Job broke silence and cursed on his day.' After this, i.e. after seven days and nights of silence, Job curses the day of his birth and his whole existence. How is this possible? The prologue is always talking about *barak*, blessing or saying goodbye to God, and Job has just been described as the one who does not curse despite all his misery. What has happened? Has Job changed his tack? It seems like it. Job does not curse God, but certainly rages against his own life and the wretched life of all human beings. He curses or wishes away *(qalal)* his existence and wishes that he had never seen the light of day.

The structure of the monologue

The curse that Job utters is a really strange one. Job curses something that has taken place in the distant past, but does not expect that his life will be reversed. Rather, he turns inwards and concentrates on the emotions which are seething within him. He gives vent to them in a passionate lament. Here he is not addressing anyone in particular, either his friends or God. This is more of an interior monologue of which only the narrator knows (and therefore so do we). In the first part of his monologue (3.1–10), Job makes statements which are between a wish and a lament. That is strange, because in general a wish relates to the future and a lament to the past. Hence the remarkable translation of the first verses: 'May the days from the past not have taken place!' Job tries to sweep away his present and future by undoing his past. Had he not been born, this misery would never have come upon him. Job alternately mentions the day and the night of his birth. He wishes that a conception had never taken place in the night. He wants the night in which his mother conceived him never to have existed; he wishes that God had kept the door of his mother's womb locked. He would have wanted God not to have made any dawn follow this night, to have forgotten to give any light to this day. The bitterness rises from these sentences like dense smoke. The reader cannot see Job's swearing, but as it were smell the stink of it.

After this first part, in the two following laments (3.11–19; 3.20–23) the furious questions roll out one after another, always beginning with 'Why?'. 'Dammit, why me, why not someone else? Why didn't I die at my birth, then I would now have rest. Why didn't I die before my birth? Then at least I would never have lived, and I would be better off .' The death which he refused when his wife gave him the choice now seems to him to be far more attractive than life. In the second lament Job no longer keeps to himself but extends his lament to all human beings. These words, too, are introduced with a 'Why?'. 'Why must other people, too, who have just as much suffering as I do, remain alive? They, too, would prefer to be dead, just like me.' And then follows the key question in 3.23: 'Why has God given life to human beings, a life of which they cannot see the meaning? In God's name, what is that good for?'

Only in the last part of his monologue (3.24–26) does Job speak again for himself. This emerges from the fact that in these three verses the terms 'I' or 'me' occur six times. Sorrow has become his food and tears his daily drink. He is still only a consumer of sighs and laments. He has lost his rest and he has fallen prey to total confusion.

The theme of the monologue

It's a Saturday evening, five minutes before the news begins. We put on the television and see the following film.

It's a bright summer day. A sprinkler is spraying on a green lawn in front of an attractive bungalow. Two children, fair-haired and healthy, are playing there. A friendly dog romps around them, barking. Father drives up in his shiny estate car. The children greet him joyfully. A woman who is pretty as a picture comes out of the house and kisses her husband, who is equally smart. They enter the house, but soon afterwards emerge to begin a happy barbecue. They go in and out with nibbles, meat and salads, plastic plates and napkins. A parasol is set up above the table and the eating can begin. Suddenly a ball flies through the garden. It makes a direct hit on the shaky barbecue. The barbecue falls over, and the fire rapidly spreads all around. The tablecloth catches fire, as does the new garden furniture. The people are also threatened. The youngest child stumbles, catches her foot and can't get it free. She shrieks, because her hair catches fire. The father tries to put out the fire but can't. He clasps his daughter in his arms, and waits hopelessly for the ambulance. Unfortunately, the fire is spreading so quickly that the flames reach the kitchen and, because unfortunately the gas furnace was still on, destroys it all. The fire engine, which fortunately comes very quickly, rams the nice estate car. Experts as they are, the firemen put out the fire quickly, but as a result of the water damage the house looks more like a dripping tree than a dwelling.

In a few seconds the idyll of this family has been changed into a forlorn hope. Fortunately the insurance man is there . . . and promotes a fire insurance which will cover us against all this.

You can see this film as a parody of Job 1, 2 and 3; all that is missing in these chapters is the insurance man. In the land of Uz, which sounds very like the land of Oz, long ago and far away, a man called Job lived in a dreamlike perfection: very rich, extremely pious, with an ideal number of children and very large numbers of cattle. It seems almost too attractive, an illusory world of prosperity and happiness, with Job as the perfect moral man. The blows are as much a nightmare as the prosperity is a dream. In a moment perfect happiness is followed by complete misery.

Job seems at first to remain on his feet. 'Nothing to be done about it, a bit of trouble, those who accept good must also accept bad.' But under his skin the blow has hit hard. Through the skin the satan has penetrated deep into his body. Someone who believed so much in a fair balance, arrived at through rules and good deeds in accordance with them, and then sees his world collapse despite that good behaviour, can no longer return to this ideal order. The foundations on which his world was built have been undermined. At first Job does not yet seem to realize that, but gradually it gets through to him. The cohesion of his world has been permanently destroyed and it has fallen apart. The old familiar set of values which he followed has disappeared, together with the prosperity which he had deserved by keeping the rules. The future no longer offers him any help; at most a speedy death. But there is a difference between the modern man, the outsider characterized by absurdity as Camus described him, and the person of Job. That difference is faith in God. If God did not exist for Job, as God no longer exists for many people now, the problems which appear in the book of Job would not arise. In that case life would be absurd. But Job believes that God does exist and that God is righteous, and therefore he must look at the questions which this raises and confront the contingency of existence with the incomprehensible, transcendent God.

This is evident right from the very beginning of the monologue. Job's own unmerited suffering has put him in a position to look further and to recognize that there is no meaning or significance in his existence. He see clearly that this is not just his own individual fate, but the universal fate of all human beings. The whole of humankind is called to a painful and meaningless existence. As creatures, human beings are simply thrown into existence by God, and God can do what he wants with them. He himself has been hurled from a prosperity which he thought that he had merited by acting justly into a suffering the reason for which he cannot see. Prosperity and suffering are both assigned to human beings equally arbitrarily. Good people suffer just as much as bad people; possibly they suffer even more.

What must a person then still believe? The only rules that Job knew were the rules of traditional faith. He has kept these rules, but that has been no use. These rules, too, are meaningless and give no sense to life. If existence itself no longer offers any pleasure but only misery and bitterness, then one had better give it up. The only prospect then is an end to life, since life itself is simply frightening. For Job these questions weigh all the more heavily because he cannot postpone the problems until after death, as became customary in later Christian tradition. He recognizes no life after death and therefore must give the problems their head here and now. Thus Job's present misery becomes the focus of his view of human existence. Only an acute sense of the past exists for him.

The hinge between prologue and dialogue

The opposition between Job's soliloquy and the pious Job of the prologue seems unbridgeable. What links this rebel with the tranquil Job? In the prologue we had already seen that Job's faith and tranquilllity were beginning to show some cracks. Now these cracks have become quite visible divisions. Job's accepting look upwards towards God in chapter 1, which is gradually changed into a more doubting look around him in chapter 2, has now in chapter 3 become a desperate look into the gaping abyss of his innermost depths. The friends will begin to react to this last situation in the following chapters. Job's monologue functions so to speak as a hinge between the preceding prologue and the dialogues which follow. That applies not only to the perspective and the emotional loading, but also to a number of other elements which reinforce the function of Job 3 as a hinge between Job 1–2 and Job 4ff.

A first link is formed by the expression 'hedge around' or 'surround with a hedge' which appears both in the prologue and in Job's monologue, and makes the transition to the dialogue possible. In 1.9–10 the satan says to God,

'Is Job's fear of God disinterested?
Haven't you put a hedge around him and his house and all that he has?
Haven't you blessed the work of his hands,
so that his possessions have increased over the land?'

In Job's monologue the term 'hedge around' returns when in 3.23 Job says:

'(Why give life) to a human being whose way is hidden;
now that God has hedged him in?'

In the prologue the satan speaks in heaven and says that God protects Job with a hedge. According to the satan, with this hedge God ensures that Job keeps the good and is protected against all evil. By contrast, in the monologue Job is speaking on earth and claims that God has surrounded human life with a hedge, so that people cannot see further than the present and cannot tell what is coming to them. Here Job is protesting because as a human being he feels imprisoned and cut off from an overall view. He complains that since he does not know the goal of his life, he cannot estimate its significance or meaning. Job is thus arguing from a human perspective and evaluating this hedge in a negative way, since he wants to survey his whole life. The satan argues as one of the heavenly beings who does survey the universe. He can take a positive view of the hedge around Job's life: it is God's protection against negative influences. So the word 'hedge around' offers two pictures which as it were mirror each other: it portrays something that offers protection and thus keeps out the bad (the satan), or something that forms a barrier and thus keeps out the good (Job). The duality or ambiguity of the term 'hedge around' makes it possible to move from the positive use of the term in the prologue through the negative use of 'hedge around' in the monologue to the dialogues between Job and his friends and between Job and God. In them an important subject for discussion will be both whether human beings are enclosed in their own world and context, and also whether they can see sufficiently beyond to give meaning to their existence.

Another hinge is the term 'fear'. In the prologue Job is repeatedly called 'godfearing'. We saw that there is a degree of tension in this godfearing, to the extent that Job is afraid that he himself or his children are committing errors (1.5). In the monologue precisely this thread is taken up again in 3.25:

> 'For what I most fear has comes upon me,
> and what I dreaded has befallen me.'

The ambiguity in Job's piety mentioned in the prologue is thus confirmed by Job himself. Modern educationalists and psychologists would now call Job's behaviour 'a positive anxiety about failure': Job is afraid of making mistakes, and wants to do everything perfectly. And some would say that in terms of psychoanalysis the figure of the satan is a projection of the conflict that is taking place in Job himself. The prologue then depicts Job's anxiety in the form a conflict that is being played out outside him, and the monologue in the form a conflict that is being played out within him. In the Hebrew text the ambiguity of the prologue over Job's piety is exploited to the full. Job's first scrupulous fear of God, full of blessing and without cursing, forms the breeding ground for the later doubt, expressed as not blessing and not cursing God in 2.10. Now that the fear has become reality, Job's doubt turns into a negative wish. He does not bless God, does not curse him, but wishes away or curses his own life. For Eliphaz this negative wish is the reason to begin speaking after the long silence. Job, who has the reputation of being so godfearing, is wishing his life away and that is not allowed, says Eliphaz. The other friends tell him this in even stronger terms.

The names that Job gives to God also function as an element in his monologue which makes possible the gradual transition from the prologue to the dialogues that are to come. In the first part of the prologue Job prays directly to God with the name YHWH (1.21). After that, in the second part of the prologue and in reaction to his wife's question he calls him *ha-elohim*, 'the god' or 'the deity'; this indicates that his distance from God has become greater. In his monologue Job twice uses the term *eloah,*

'God'. The first time (3.4) he speaks of 'God on high', i.e. of a God whom he feels to be far away. The second time (3.23) he calls God the one who has barred the way for human beings by a hedge. The hedge not only prevents human beings from seeing their own way, but also seems to hinder contact with or belief in God. If you cannot get an overall picture, how do you know whether God is just? A kind of fence or partition seems to have been erected between God and human beings. If in the prologue Job thought that he still had some view of God, in Job 3 he has lost it. In the following dialogues between Job and his friends God will alternately be called God, *elohim, el* or *eloah* and sometimes also *shaddai*, the Most High. Thus the distance from God which Job feels for the first time in 2.10 and to an even greater degree in the monologue has become the starting point for discussion with the friends.

From rest to unrest

After his Stoic reaction in the prologue, Job shows his emotions in his monologue. He is so desperate that he begins passionately to long for death.

> 'Why did I not die at birth? . . .
> Then I would now be lying down, be at rest, sleeping, undisturbed,
> next to kings and princes of this world,
> who built ruins for themselves,
> or next to rulers who had gold,
> and filled their houses with silver . . .
> There the evildoers cease from their pursuits;
> there those whose strength is exhausted rest.
> There prisoners are at ease together . . .
> The small and the great are there alike
> and the slave is free from his master' (3.11–19).

After a series of negative wishes about his birth and life, Job expresses his longing for death. He conjures up for us a picture of the underworld as an oasis of rest. The luxury and prosperity that are really expected of life are now all attributed to death. Job conjures up the picture of death as an idyllic place. It is peaceful there; there are no longer any differences between poor and rich, servant and master. He describes death as a new heaven and a new èarth. It seems a paradox that he now describes everything that can make life worth living, rest, peace and equality, as properties of death. This expresses *par excellence* the despair that Job feels. The core of this despair comes at the end of his soliloquy (3.25–26):

> 'For what I most feared has come upon me,
> and what I dreaded has befallen me.
> I have no happiness, no rest,
> no peace, only ongoing unrest.'

What did Job always fear and what was he afraid of when in 1.5 he offered purificatory sacrifices for his children? Was he afraid of losing God's favour and thus also his prosperity, as the satan suggests? Or was he afraid of suffering? Job himself gives the answer. The loss of rest, anxiety about chaos or sheer confusion in which nothing is any longer what it seems, that is what he was afraid of, and that is what he had wanted to avoid by an exemplary life of faith. Looking back to the first verses of the prologue, we are struck by the tranquillity and secure ordering of everything: there is great regularity and rest, an existence regulated by piety and the fixed rhythms of festivals and sacrifices. This was the pattern of Job's life, which has now been lost. Job's last words speak volumes: from today confusion or unrest characterize his existence.

Job shows his emotions in this monologue and then ends with these verses. The emotions are raw and devour him within. He curses himself and the world. This is the lot of someone who lived in a world of security, a world in which there were order, rest and cohesion. In the monologue the negative layer, the anxiety under Job's piety, which was woven in the prologue, is spun out into an inner web of unrest and confusion. This confusion has attacked Job in all his fibres. This poem is not a reflection on death or human suffering in the world. It is about the drama of this particular person who is afflicted by the uttermost despair. We as readers are invited to dive into this pool of feelings, and run the risk of being drawn into the whirlpool that is called despair.

The Three Dialogues: Job 4–27

The dialogues: dull?

Challenged by Job's monologue, his friends enter into discussion with him. Not once or twice, but time and again they put their views to him, and each time Job reacts afresh. More than thirty chapters (including Elihu's speech) are devoted to this. The friends keep running through the same arguments and keep scoring the same points. All this makes the long section with the dialogues exhausting. Standpoint follows standpoint, repetition follows repetition. The lack of alternation and dramatic development is characteristic of the content of the dialogues themselves. Everything is static, nothing happens, and no one changes their views. Despite all their efforts the friends get nowhere. The exhausting repetitions, the superabundance of standpoints and observations, the points of discussion exhaust Job and also exhaust the reader. The friends hope that Job will say, 'Just stop, you're right, that's enough.' The reader can perhaps be softened up, but not Job. You could say, with an allusion to God, 'Have you seen Job, no one is as tenacious and stubborn as he is?'

People are sitting in a meeting in a smoky room. One man with a harsh voice can dominate and direct the meeting simply by the loudness of his voice. Another is better at achieving his ends with flattery and gentle comments. Someone else speaks well and uses rhetoric, which enables him to convince other people. And people are sitting there who don't attract attention but listen all the more attentively and check closely. In a meeting full of such people, all are 'of course' intent on their own goals, but in addition they themselves are almost more important as a goal. Therefore the discussions are often not focussed on the substance of the matter but on the convictions of others, being right and scoring points. Every means is used to gain others to one's own standpoint, to win them over and to manipulate them.

Something of the same kind also happens in the dialogues between Job and his friends. The tone and the rhetoric make up half the content. Job's friends sympahtize with him, and all three have the same aim, to comfort Job. At the same time they try to win him over to their own view. At first they all still hope that they will succeed and use friendly rhetorical means; later they come with the heavy artillery.

Thus we have Eliphaz, the first to open his mouth. He tries the way of friendliness and honesty. He begins modestly: 'Job, I hope you don't mind if I begin to talk to you. Now that I've heard you I can't keep silent any longer.' He wants to reassure Job and make him receptive: 'I know very well how many people you've helped, who knew no better and lost their way.' But very quickly he gets to what he really wants to say and combines his praise with a rebuke: 'But now that you yourself are affected, you're panicking. That disappoints me. Have you lost all the strength that you showed to others?' Finally he offers his help. 'Just think, have you ever seen any innocent person who lost his possessions? Have righteous people ever perished? Only people who have deserved it perish by God's hand; all the others are protected by him. You've done nothing bad and so you've nothing to fear.' Rebuke and reassurance go hand in hand. He throws in the moral superiority of his whole wisdom, his status as the grand old man, to bring Job back into the fold.

Bildad, the second friend, speaks much more directly and his tone is less cautious. In reaction to Eliphaz, Job had said that his words had flown away in the wind. Bildad takes this up frankly and grants Job the wind: 'Job, your words are empty words, as fleeting as the wind.' Bildad speaks with more certainty than Eliphaz. He thinks that he knows better than Job. Like Eliphaz, he believes that suffering is a punishment for sin. Thus if Job has lived a good life, he will not perish as a result of all this. Eliphaz had still said that Job didn't need to be afraid, because he had done nothing bad. By contrast, Bildad speaks conditionally: 'If Job hasn't sinned, then he needn't be afraid.' Bildad's rhetoric is well thought out. If anyone were to criticize him later, he could say, 'I didn't say that Job had sinned, only that "if he has sins, then he will be punished".' Bildad is to be compared with the negotiator who can always find some loophole. But in fact he goes one stage further than Eliphaz, who begins from Job's innocence. By leaving open the question whether or not Job is innocent, he reckons with the possibility of guilt. In fact Bildad's view, is, 'Where there's smoke there's fire. Job is suffering and so he may well have sinned.'

Zophar, finally, is almost aggressive, 'You complain, blaspheme and more. You silence other people. You should have been silenced yourself.' His tone is more striking than what he says, since he is simply taking up the views of the two previous speakers. Suffering comes from sin; Job is suffering and is thus a sinner. If Job doesn't see this, he is stone blind. Eliphaz says that no one is without error. Bildad had spoken about the sin of Job's children. Zophar accuses Job of having himself sinned: 'It's your own fault. In fact Job is suffering less than he deserves from his guilt. He should be grateful to God for that!' Splendid to have some one who comforts you like that!

Someone who is having a hard time in a meeting will eventually fall silent. Whether convinced or not, you can't keep moaning on for ever. However, for Job more is at stake than is the case in most meetings and he doesn't fall silent. On the contrary, his reactions get longer and longer by comparison with the previous speakers. Is Job therefore to be regarded as a persistent bore or someone who is set on showing that he is right? It seems, rather, as if Job is so driven by what he has experienced that it makes no difference to him how people see him. Epithets like 'pigheaded', 'bore', 'tedious' are nothing to him compared with his misery. He stands up for his own life and questions, and keeps putting them more and more sharply. He doesn't care if he puts his friends off. And the narrator, who takes his side, also doesn't care whether he holds the reader's attention or puts them off by the length of the dialouges. He and Job are concerned with important matters.

Or fascinating?

The speeches are long, but whether they are also dull depends on our pattern of expectation. If we expect a story with a clear line, preferably with an interesting plot or dénouement, then we shall be disappointed. Only the prologue and the epilogue have a narrative character. There is a line in them which indicates why everything has happened to Job and how he reacts. There is no story in the dialogues, and the line has also disappeared. The form and content have become those of poetry. The dialogues present as it were a torrent of questions and answers, doubts and thoughts, assertions and denials. The ambiguity characteristic of poetry fits the toing and froing of the four men better than a straightforward story. The succession of arguments and counter-arguments shows that it is not possible to give clear or simple answers to questions about suffering, about God and human beings. Almost every part of the dialogues is a challenge to the reader to investigate these elementary questions.

Out of the crisis of his life Job puts his questions, and the friends react to them. They experience all this very intensively and therefore in a sense the dialogue is to be seen as a psychological drama. But the question then is whether we can also perceive a character development or psychological growth in the speaker. Probably progression and poetry are not the best combination conceivable. Moreover progress presupposes a retrospect from a situation in which everything is already past. These dialogues do not begin from a vantage point, but take place in the thick of the situation, during the crisis itself. Those who are in the thick of things cannot play God; they just see how things develop.

The main theme of the dialogues

The starting point of the friends in the dialogues is a picture of God handed on and written down in the centuries before them, one which even after them has been adhered to for centuries, down to the present day. In this view, along with creation God has spun a great web of causality over the world. Human beings live within this web, and the result of their lives depends on what they do. If they do good, they are rewarded; if they do evil, they are punished. On the basis of this causality people have their own fate and indirectly God in their hands, since God observes this relation between cause and effect. So human logic is used as a criterion for God. From this point of view God is then called just.

The friends, who have really come to comfort Job, attack him from the perspective of this view of the world and of God. They claim that their view of God is based both on the tradition and on perceived reality. But they do not listen to Job's reality. Job repeatedly says to them, 'If only you would listen to me. Reality does not correspond with your theory. The world is not governed by the principle of moral retribution, since there is no just or fair distribution of justice and injustice in the world. You can hang on to this view only because you give a misleading interpretation of the world and adapt the world to theory. You whitewash the dark side of life with lies. Because of this mendacious view of the world you develop a picture of God which can only be a false picture of God.' Here Job is unmasking a form of fraudulent belief which often occurs. The opposition between the world which is experienced and the traditional view is overgrown with deceit, since the doctrine is not applied to reality, but reality to the doctrine. However, we can say with Job that true faith has nothing to do with fraud. Believing means not closing your eyes to reality and blindly following the traditional view of God and the world, even if they no longer correspond with reality as it is experienced. Far less does believing mean that you can impose your own rules on God and then call him just.

Job does not just present his own, different, view of the world. What is crucial is his rejection of the principle that underlies the arguments of the friends. They argue from perceived reality to its cause and declare that Job's suffering is the consequence of sins committed earlier. Job rejects this so-called logic of everyday thought. He doesn't say that he hasn't made any mistakes, but he denies categorically that his suffering results from his behaviour. The arguments of the friends are based on a theory or doctrine. Job's arguments in the conversations with his friends are based on his life, his experience and his person.

The following poem by Cees Nooteboom can serve as a comparison:

Scholasticism

This is the oldest conversation on earth
The rhetoric of water
exploding on the dogma of stone.

But at the invisible end
only the poet knows how it all turns out.
He dips his pen in the rocks
and writes on a tablet
of foam.

In the conversations with his friends the rhetoric of life, the existential experiences, the alternations of suffering and joy which Job experiences keep clashing with the traditional view of how everything fits together. In the view of the friends, reality must be adapted to doctrine. Moreover this doctrine can never be falsified. The principle of justice in the form of moral retribution has thus become a real dogma written in stone. There is a striking similarity between the second couplet of the poem above and the last part of the book of Job (Job 38–42). At the invisible end it is only God who knows how things turn out and rewrites the rocks of doctrine as a theory of life. But above all there is the author of the book of Job, who has given form to all this in such a way that we as readers become aware of this struggle between fossilized dogma and living water.

Before we get to this end and can listen to God's own statements we first take part in all the disputes and arguments between Job and his friends. As the discussions progress, the tension between them becomes greater. When the friends speak of God's omnipotence, providence and wisdom, Job remarks: 'Certainly, God is powerful and wise, but his power is brute force, his wisdom cunning and he himself is a Mafia boss. God as I experience him in my existence seems more like a gangster than a just and loving father.' Unlike the friends, Job feels that he is a target of this trigger-happy God. For Job, the conversations with his friends are not optional, the exposition of a poem or a discussion over a drink. For him this is a life-and-death conversation. Moreover his description of God and the world quickly becomes an accusation in which he challenges God. Therefore Job's dispute with his friends turns into a charge on which he brings God to court. In the last chapters of the dialogue Job no longer mentions his friends. They have disappeared from the scene. Job asks to talk to the big boss himself. He succeeds in doing so, and when they meet, they are the only actors on the stage.

You cannot read the dialogues in the book of Job without getting an impression of Job's picture of God: a gangster who is constantly after him. For us, this God is far more gripping than the theological abstraction of the friends. So one can say that the dialogues are not only about how human beings can live in a world full of misery, but at the same time are also about God himself. Moreover the question who God is, an idea, an abstraction, a projection or someone whom you can experience, plays an important role here. In their conversations, Job and his friends give various answers to this question and develop divergent pictures of God. This is an important theme in the book of Job, as was already indicated in the prologue: how is a connection to be made between the experienced contingency of existence and the (various pictures of) the transcendent God? I have described the friends' answer as the doctrine of moral retribution, which human beings and God recognize. For them the relationship between God and the world is fixed in the logic of causality. Job's answer is in the first instance more a question and a request for clarification. Gradually his opposition to the doctrine adhered to by his friends increases and his thought about God undergoes a change.

Job's friends

You should be a friend of Job's. You come a long way with good intentions. You spend seven days and nights sitting with him, try to support him, really sympathize with him. You go on listening and talking, since Job won't stop. He is indefatigable. But as a good friend you don't give up. You contribute what you know, from your faith, what you've always taught, and that is what Job, too, had previously told others. After days and nights of talking you've got nowhere. You sit there thinking only of going back home. Then you get told off. Job is annoyed that you haven't helped him, God says that what you've said was wrong, and afterwards you go down in history as a kind of fool. Small thanks. Since then Job's friends have become the prototypes of how not to do things. So they are often described like this:

Eliphaz is the kind of person who begins by saying that he loves you so much and is therefore anxious to persuade you to accept his way of seeing things. He is someone who begins his prayers with, 'Lord, I just want to ask you . . .', and then it emerges from his 'just' that the Lord has to dispose the whole universe in accordance with his interests.

In this view Bildad is a follower of religious authority. He has a sticker on the back of his car which says, 'God says it, I believe it, and that's that.' Teach him to know human nature! He knows it all. He knows that AIDS is the well-deserved punishment for transgressions committed earlier, and that even satisfies him: justice at last! Moreover he says to Job, 'Your children must have sinned. God has punished them so that they perished.'

Along these lines, Zophar is described as a Bildad who has studied. He shares Bildad's rigid standpoint about punishment and sin, but he has learned to rationalize everything. Zophar takes out his pipe and tells Job, who at this moment is busy scraping his sores with a potsherd, 'the whole thing is complicated, very complicated.' Zophar has decided that Job's whole problem is a lack of understanding. Job doesn't understand that he is a sinner. Zophar puts his chin on his hand and benevolently asks, 'Job, how is it possible that you don't see this? How can I make it clear to you?' He instructs Job in the theory of justice, but he is doubtful whether Job is capable of understanding it.

Here, too, so far a negative picture of the friends has been sketched out, as if they were merely conservative dogmatists. But I think to myself that I am usually more like Job's friends than like Job himself. How often does someone come to appeal

to you? Someone who has just been divorced and is now completely at a loss, someone who has lost a child? They come to
you and after a while you begin to speak in terms of your own
particular view of life. Not because you're such an expert, but
preciesely because you aren't. So you refer to what you've
learned or experienced as good or valuable. You use your values
as a criterion for judging things and giving well-meant advice.
Of course your views aren't as rigid as the doctrine of moral
retribution sketched out above; who wants to embody a fossilized doctrine? But you have to do something. You can't stop at
the concrete instance of the individual sufferer who is sitting
beside you. And that is precisely what the friends do. They
really sympathize. They compare what Job says with what they
themselves think, and get trampled on for their pains.

However, all these approaches are one-sided, whether they
caricature the friends and reject their positions and standpoints,
or identify completely with them. One cannot act as if Job is
always right in the dialogues and the friends are simply wrong.
Everyone says something good and something bad. They learn
from one another, and in this sense there is a real dialogue.
I don't think that we have to pin everything on God's one little
remark in 42.7 when he says that the friends have not spoken
well but Job has. We can't apply that retrospectively to everything and thus write off the whole book and all the conversations. No, this remark by God must be put in its own place and
understood after the dialogues and God's speech. The digressions in the dialogues are real digressions and therefore Job's
friends are to be regarded as friends and catalysts in the
whole process of growth in Job's faith. They cannot be made
caricatures of friends like those in the example above.

The First Round of Conversation between Eliphaz and Job: Job 4–7

Eliphaz is the first of Job's friends to speak after Job's monologue. As readers we are soon impressed by the dignity, sobriety and reticence with which Eliphaz says things in reply to the vigorous, one could almost say uncontrolled outburst by Job in chapter 3. Eliphaz's speech contains different elements. Sometimes he is encouraging (4.2–11), then visionary (4.12–21), then he rebukes (5.1–7) or gives hope (5.8–27). Moreover his speech contains a great many ambiguities and double meanings which make it possible to listen to this conversation in two ways, through the ears of Eliphaz and through the ears of Job.

Eliphaz's perspective

We come to Job and I'm horrified. How terrible he looks! I ask myself how we can support him in this sorry time. First the three of us go to sit with him by the heap of ashes. For seven days and seven nights. In that way we at least make it clear that we aren't leaving him in the lurch. But when Job engages in an outburst, I can't keep silent any longer. Fortunately during our long silence I've had plenty of time to think everything over. When I open my mouth I've carefully considered what to say: 'Have courage! Don't you remember how you yourself have always helped others? Don't lose courage now that you yourself are afflicted, and don't panic.' It isn't easy for me to utter this encouragement. I know what a believer Job has always been. He can draw courage from his faith and therefore he continues to trust in the future. This (4.6) is the nub of what I want to say:

'Is not your fear of God your confidence
and the integrity of your life your hope?'

I begin immediately by referring to Job's piety and integrity. No one lives such a good life as he does. Precisely because I believe in justice and know that God guarantees that human beings will be recompensed in accordance with their behaviour, good or bad, Job can be reassured. At the end of my argument (in 5.17–26), I emphasize this once again. Surely I'm giving him a developed picture of a hopeful future?

> 'Behold, happy is the man whom God reproves!
> Moreover do not despise the chastening of the Almighty.
> He wounds, but he also binds up;
> he smites, but his hands heal . . .
> You shall know that all is well in your tent,
> count your cattle, and you will miss nothing.
> You shall know also that your descendants shall be many,
> and your offspring as the grass of the earth.'

Job sits in the dirt and thinks that things will always be as bad as this, but I know that they will get better. He will have more children, acquire more possessions and share in the good life. He must simply hold on. However, I cannot ignore his earlier outburst and protest, so along with the encouragement and comfort I must make it clear that Job's outburst is unfair and that he is being foolish. Still, I don't say this bluntly, but cautiously and compassionately. I'm not bothered that Job has made mistakes. No one is perfect, everyone makes mistakes. In the night vision that I had recently, I saw how all human beings fall short, and even angels do now and then. I'm glad that I can tell him about this wonderful vision. In this way I'm in a position to make it clear to him that as a human being he can expect suffering, not because he is a greater sinner than others, but because he is a creature. His sinfulness lies in his createdness. But precisely because I believe in justice, in a moral ordering of the world by God, I can say to Job from the bottom of my heart: 'As an innocent man, what do you have to fear? Precisely because there is justice, you can have hope and good courage.' I only want to say that I do my best to be as honest as possible to Job, and refrain from any direct or personal attack on him. He hasn't deserved that, for he is truly a great and pious man.

Job's perspective

Nice friends I've got. First everything went well. They came and sat with me and fortunately said nothing, no false words of comfort, no hypocrisy. But hardly had I opened my mouth to complain to God about all my unmerited suffering when Eliphaz began. After a few words of comfort, he said, 'Those who sow evil, will reap misery' (4.8). Does he mean that I am now reaping misery because I was formerly wrong or, in his words, sowed badly? Of course it may well be that he simply wanted to indicate the other side of the coin. Perhaps he only wanted to say that just as all will go well with the innocent, so it will go badly with the unjust. Perhaps I shouldn't take him too seriously; perhaps he just meant it as a warning. But what a stupid thing to say, just as I'm feeling overwhelmed with how badly things are going for me!

However, Eliphaz is unstoppable, and he chastizes me as though I were a small child or a fool. He criticizes me and says that my way of talking about God is completely unacceptable. I believe that he is afraid that I am rebelling against God and will curse him. He should know me better than that. He should know that to curse God is the last thing that I shall ever do. Despite all his so-called sympathy, Eliphaz doubts me in a very basic way. That emerges from what he says to me next:

> 'Call now! Is there anyone who will answer you?
> To which of the holy ones will you turn?
> The fool dies by his own offensiveness,
> the simple perishes through his indignation.
> I myself have seen the fool taking root,
> but suddenly I cursed his dwelling.
> His sons are forsaken,
> they have no help,
> they have no rights in the gate . . .
> For affliction does not come from the dust,
> nor does trouble sprout from the ground.
> No, all wretchedness comes from man,
> as the sparks fly upward (5.1–7)

Am I like one of the fools Eliphaz talks about? It looks like it, given that like me, the person he is talking about has 'taken root' and then lost his dwelling. And he may well be referring to my sons when he speaks of the sons of the fool who have no help. But his final sentence is the last straw: 'For affliction does not come from the dust, no, all wretchedness comes from man.' What is he thinking of? Is he saying that I have myself to thank for all my misery? That's great. I'll tell him. I didn't think he could do this to me. His whole account is meant to blame me for my own unhappiness, and that's just not true.

When I think about it, what am I to do with his vision? I like its content, but the problem with people who think that their ideas are supported by a divine vision is that they are cruel, quite unintentionally. Because they are sure of their authority and the universal applicability of the insights that have been revealed to them, they aren't in a position to put themselves in the situation of others and see their problems. They may have sympathy, but it's an abstract sympathy which doesn't in fact help. That's also the case with Eliphaz. He isn't capable of assimilating ideas and feelings which differ from his own. That's why his generalizations are so deadly, because they reduce my suffering to universal human suffering.

I could have forgiven him all his talk had he not come up with that last so-called comforting statement: 'You shall know that all is well in your tent, you shall know also that your descendants shall be many' (5.24–25). To talk about numerous descendants to someone who has just lost all his children is stupid. He makes me cross with his splendid statement, 'Then no one will be hungry any more, there will be no more stones in the field, there will be no more wild animals and peace will prevail. Your numerous descendants will have a rich and full life' (5.23ff.). To say this to someone who has just lost everything, is that comfort? It makes me want to say, 'You know what you can do with your nice talk.'

Ambiguity in Eliphaz's speech

Eliphaz expresses himself in a way that can very easily lead to misunderstanding. Not once but many times he uses words, sentences and comparisons which can be understood both positively and negatively at the same time. He seems almost to be doing it on purpose. He speaks in an encouraging and comforting way and he speaks about a hopeful future. But if you look closely at these comforting words and the picture of the future which he presents, that picture seems to be precisely the opposite of the actual situation in which Job finds himself. As a result Job begins to feel his pain even worse and his complaint about Eliphaz is understandable.

Confronted with the positive and negative sides and the two levels in Eliphaz's speech, many interpretations and readings are possible for the reader. We can either take the positive aspects of Eliphaz's argument more seriously than the negative, or give preference to the negative sides. Job's reaction to Eliphaz in chapters 6 and 7 will probably make us inclined to opt for the second possibility and thus come down in favour of Job and against Eliphaz. Like Job, we will then regard Eliphaz's speech as comfort in the form of a sweeping generalization and react with, 'Nicely said, but it doesn't get me any further.' But we can also opt for a third reading. We can think that Eliphaz means well for Job and that his comfort is honestly intended, and yet be put off by Eliphaz's lack of real sympathy. In this way we note the ambiguity in Eliphaz's argument and respect the positive elements as well as the negative ones.

Eliphaz's vision

'A word came to me secretly,
my ear received the whisper of it.
In the restless visions of the night,
when deep sleep overtakes men,
terror and anxiety seized me,
and made all my bones shake.
A wind blew across my face;
a stormwind made my flesh creep.
A figure stood there, unrecognizable,
a face before my eyes,
and I heard a voice:
"Can a mortal man be righteous before God,
Can a man be pure in the eyes of his maker?
If God cannot trust his own servants,

and still finds faults in his angels,
how much more in those who dwell in houses of clay,
who come from dust and are crushed like moths,
destroyed before it is morning and evening,
perished for ever, without anyone noticing.
Their tent cord is plucked up within them
and they die without wisdom" ' (4.12–21).

To show that he has an authentically divine vision, Eliphaz gives a long introduction in which he describes how he heard a divine voice in the night. We can take this in two ways. Either the vision is inauthentic and has been thought up by Eliphaz to elevate his own opinion to a universal truth. Or Eliphaz has gained knowledge of a divine word in an extraordinary way. A decision can be made only by looking at the content of the vision.

The emphasis on human fragility is part of the vision, but it plays a subordinate role. The main issue is whether human beings can be righteous before God. The voice in the vision therefore immediately begins with the question whether a mortal can be pure and righteous in the eyes of his maker (4.17). Job and his friends are all agreed on the incapacity of human beings and the enormous power and might of God. But in addition the friends assert that God treats good or innocent people better than bad people. Against that Job says that destruction and pain affect both groups. From Job's perspective the divine saying in this vision provides support for his own experience. Since no one can claim complete innocence, no one can expect justice from God either. Eliphaz could have drawn his mistaken conclusions from this. Thus it is indirectly evident that Eliphaz is handing on an authentic saying of God which confirms Job's view rather than his own.

Through that vision Job perceives something very important. From this divine saying he can infer God's freedom. God is free in his treatment of the guilty and the innocent. Previously, just like his friends, Job began from the traditional view that God blesses the righteous and punishes the wicked. But in the light of his own suffering he is now forced to see how untenable this view is. The vision confirms Job's doubt whether there is such a simple mechanical formula through which the just person will ultimately find happiness and the wicked person unhappiness.

Since Job himself is experiencing physically that innocence and suffering can occur in a person at the same time, he can begin to see that God's treatment of human beings in this vision accords with his experience of the world. He is gradually compelled to give up his theory for an attitude in which he recognizes that he can no longer see everything. Such a standpoint would mean that only God can survey everything and that God is essentially free to act in accordance with his insights.

This vision does not give any other reasons why good people suffer innocently. A partial explanation can be that God has angels who also make mistakes and therefore do not carry out God's commands as they should (4.18). Another cause of injustice is the way in which people treat one another. They are even more untrustworthy than the angels. Through this vision Job can gain an important insight and discover that not only is God free to do and allow what he wills, but human beings are also free. We really could have known that earlier. The prologue, Job 1 and 2, describes how Sabaeans and Chaldaeans steal Job's animals and kill his servants. These thieves and murderers are human beings, and these human beings do what they want. After that, fire from heaven and a storm have seen to the death of Job's cattle, servants, sons and daughters. Even the natural elements are free to act. And above all there is the satan, one of God's servants, who receives permission from God to do as he likes. All creatures, from angels and human beings to animals and the elements of nature, have been given freedom at their creation to act according to their nature. They do not need permission to live, but that does not mean that God finds everything that they do good. This vision shows that sometimes the angels, but more often human beings, act in a way of which God does not approve. Nevertheless God does not withhold freedom of action and living from them. The force of this vision is that Job is confronted with a twofold freedom which determines everything and everyone: God's freedom and human freedom. Often human beings do not have enough of this freedom and want to impose their human laws and sense of justice on God. Unfortunately for them, God does not go by human criteria. God can act in ways which go above or beyond human understanding.

In this way Eliphaz's vision is helpful to Job in his efforts to understand God better. It helps him to abandon his old traditional and rational formulations and look at life as it really is. That does not mean that Job is happy with what he now hears. He would rather have had a God who quickly and efficiently secured justice for honest and righteous people. Although Job does not give up his fundamental faith in God's justice, he continues for a while to wrestle to understand God's government of the world. At this point he is not yet without insight into God's rule and motives, without trust in God's power and wisdom. With this divine saying in a nocturnal vision, Eliphaz has certainly helped Job a step further.

Job's reaction to Eliphaz

Despite the vision and the points of light in it, Job concentrates above all on the negative aspects of Eliphaz's argument and complains about the wretchedness of his present existence. He is experiencing this physically. He reacts to Eliphaz in a long complaint, a lament to God. 'My life is a breath of air, as fleeting as the wind; thus it is past.' If he is only going to be dust after his death, he will no longer be able to praise and worship God. He asks himself whether that serves God. Therefore he urgently puts to God some questions which torment him.

The first question is: 'Why give a human being life, let him grow up and surround him with care?' (7.17). Why has God devised this ingenious invention called a human being, with all those organs, sinews, bones and muscles, and surrounded this human being with care which brings suffering until death? The second question is: why does God behave in such an anxious way and spy on Job like a gaoler in all that he does? Has God nothing better to do than keep an eye on human beings all day, so that they may not even eat their meals without a feeling of guilt (7.17–19). Finally, in the third question Job comes to the nub of the matter: 'Why doesn't God forgive the shortcomings of someone who tries to live a righteous life?' (7.20–21). If God had so much difficulty in making something as complicated as human beings in the first place, if he has surrounded them with care and kept them under surveillance, why doesn't he forgive the shortcomings of those who try to do good, but as creatures cannot do better? Shouldn't God put together a better creature? Because God clearly hasn't done that, he must draw conclusions from this and forgive the mistakes and shortcomings that are human characteristics. Hence the last question that Job puts in 7.21: 'If I may have sinned, why don't you forgive my sins?'

The First Round of Conversation between Bildad and Job: Job 8–10

Friend Bildad

Bildad reacts directly to the questions which Job puts and says, 'How can you say these things? Your words are like wind; they fly away and nothing is left of them.' By this he means that Job's remarks are blasphemous. Like Eliphaz, Bildad starts from the traditional idea of a moral order based on retribution. Unlike Eliphaz, he speaks above all in legal terms. He calls God a just judge, and his view there is no doubt that God administers law in this just way. Bildad even goes far as to see God's justice demonstrated in Job's sons: they have sinned, and so they have been punished. Really he is arguing the wrong way round. Because God's sons have been punished, they will have sinned. At the same time we can see Bildad's rhetoric here. Precisely where Job himself was already having doubts about the behaviour of his sons (see 1.5), Bildad adds: 'Your sons have certainly done wrong.' To attack where doubt is nagging is a well-tried method of all intriguers.

Bildad even goes a step further. He does not apply the principle of retribution only to Job's sons but also directly to Job himself. He insinuates that things are going badly for Job because Job has done wrong in the past. The solution which he offers Job is, 'Repent and turn to God. Ask the previous generation, lend your ear to hearing what their ancestors discovered' (8.8). By this he means, 'Listen to me and those before me in the tradition. Adapt your view and experience to traditional views.' This is a familiar method of the traditionalists: whenever human experience and traditional doctrine do not fit, then experiences must be adapted to the doctrine and not the doctrine to experienced reality.

Bildad is a stricter friend than Eliphaz; he wants primarily to warn Job and not to comfort him. Job should regard the fate of his children and his own sickness as a warning. Now, while it is not too late, Job must investigate and correct his life. As a good and pious man, Bildad happily ends with a word of encouragement (8.20–22): 'Look, God does not reject an innocent man and gives no support to evildoers. He will again fill your mouth with laughter and joy shall be upon your lips . . .' In future Job will again be able to reckon on restoration and happiness, at least if he goes back to following the tradition.

Job's reaction

Bildad has certainly touched Job with his story. Job concedes that God is a just judge, almighty and seeing everything. Bildad makes Job similarly speak in legal terms: 'Anyone who wants to get into a lawsuit with God cannot answer him once in a thousand times' (9.3). Job himself also seems to believe in the doctrine of moral retribution. His opinion of the behaviour of his sons proves this, as does his reaction to Eliphaz. Things are going badly with him, he concludes, because God is imputing transgressions to him (7.19–21). Bildad's words give him the impression that as a judge God is omnipotent and that human beings are nothing: 'Though I stood on my rights, my own mouth would condemn me; though I am blameless, he would declare me guilty' (9.20). And then he refers back to himself: 'I loathe my life' (9.21).

Not only God's omnipotence smites Job, but also the complete arbitrariness with which God uses it. This God seems like a gaoler, continuously on the lookout for people making mistakes (10.14). No one can escape his gaze. If he thinks that he sees something that is not allowed, then he intervenes and punishes. Many people have such a picture of God as the great gaoler. So does Job, but he accuses this God. What kind of a gaoler is it who does not observe the legal system that he is guarding and acts in a purely arbitrary way?

Job's accusation in chapter 9 suggests God's speech from the storm in chapter 38. God begins there by asking whether Job

wants to enter into a lawsuit with him and then impresses Job
with an argument about his impressive creative power. Job does
something of the same sort here in his account. He objects to
God because he is an overwhelming and impossible opponent in
the law court. And in the middle of his legal argument, Job
mixes up his legal imagery with cosmic imagery:

'He removes mountains,
but they know it not.
He overturns them in his anger.
He shakes the earth from its place
and its pillars tremble.
He commands the sun so that it does not shine;
he seals up the stars.
He alone stretches out the heavens,
and walks over the back of the sea.
He is the maker of the Great Bear and Orion,
of the Pleiades and the circle of stars of the south.
He does great things beyond understanding,
and marvellous things without number' (9.5–10).

This is the first cosmic panorama in the book. Hitherto the
friends and Job have been concentrating on human beings. They
are not interested in what is happening around them in creation.
At this point, Job for the first time gives an indication of a wider
perspective. Here he differs from his friends. In one great
gesture Job depicts God's terrifying and arbitrary power. This
God can overturn mountains in his wrath, make the earth shake
and cover the stars. Job feels overwhelmed by this master of the
universe. God may perhaps regard himself as a great creator
and orderer, but Job experiences him more as an omnipotent
dictator. With this cosmic orientation Job differs from his
friends, though his perspective, like that of his friends, is essentially drawn from and directed towards human beings.

Arbitrariness and imagery: chinam *again*

Bildad is talking about a lawsuit in which God is always in the
right because he is right. Job is talking about a lawsuit in which
God as judge is right because he is almighty and omniscient: you

can never get past him with your understanding and power. Bildad says that 'God's order is our order and our order is God's order', but in fact he derives the divine order from the human order. By his upbringing and tradition Job tends towards the same view, but he cannot grasp why God does not then keep to this order but acts in a completely arbitrary and violent way. God is tormenting Job 'for nothing' (*chinam*). God can even destroy the cosmos 'for nothing' if he feels like it.

Thus the word *chinam*, which played such an important role in the prologue of the book of Job, reappears here in Job's reaction to his suffering (9.17). In the prologue the satan raised the question whether Job believed in God *chinam*, 'for nothing' or 'without prospect of gain' (1.9). Later it proved that God has ruined Job 'for nothing' or 'without cause and reason' (2.3). Now Job himself uses this term *chinam* to indicate God's absolute arbitrariness. Job accuses God of not just having created everything freely and for nothing, but also of having created everything without purpose, or at any rate without creation being able to see the purpose. Job says that God is tormenting him for nothing and that he is tormenting others for nothing or rewarding them for nothing. For Job everything has become completely arbitrary. For him, all the logic in creation has disappeared, and now the principle of 'one good turn deserves another' no longer seems to work. The bankruptcy of the doctrine of moral retribution is coming inexorably close, although this is Job's basic conviction and he believes in it with all his heart and soul. But Job still cannot give up this conviction. He calls for a restoration of rational principles in relations between God and human beings, for justice which is there before his eyes.

At the same time Job begins to realize that such a restoration of rationality and justice is quite impossible. For now for the first time he begins to ask whether God sees with human eyes and shares human limitations. What Job literally asks God is:

'Do you have eyes of flesh
and see as man sees?
Are your days like the days of a mortal,
and your years as the years of a human being?' (10.4–5).

Are God and human beings on speaking terms? Can they really communicate with one another on the same wavelength? At the same time this raises a related question. Can human beings really see God through human eyes? If they look at God with their eyes, what can these people see more or otherwise than what they perceive through their own eyes?

Job sits there despondent and raises the crucial question of human images of God. Job had received from his tradition an image of God as a just God, i.e. a God who judges and acts in accordance with human norms and values. He had a picture of the order of God's creation as an order which human beings can grasp with the help of tradition and reflection. Suddenly Job discovers that this order and creation cannot be grasped, that it is not tailored to human measure but overwhelms and overcomes him. The one who rejects the view that God's action is sheer caprice or *chinam* now discovers that his imagery or ideas could perhaps be *chinam* or sheer caprice. What is he then to think if everything is *chinam*, i.e. given both freely and without purpose or goal? What remains for him other than to sit down on the rubbish heap of his existence? But Job refuses to settle there. Now he is still sitting at a dead point, but this or the following nadir can prove a turning point. However, it could be a turning point when he sees the bankrupcy of the traditional view of belief in moral retribution. At present Job has not yet got this far. But he does not stop asking questions and continues his fight. It is above all this dispute which will bring him more insight than his friends. So in following the book of Job we cannot say to people, 'If only you suffer enough you will begin to believe.' It is precisely the combination of existential experience and asking questions about the consequences of it all that characterizes Job.

The First Round of Conversation with Zophar: Job 11–14

Zophar, the third friend of the trio

In chapter 10, according to his friends, Job does something unforgivable. Eliphaz and Bildad think it scarcely possible. By contrast, Zophar sees where Job has got stuck. He explicitly condemns the process that Job is going through since he understands that Job risks throwing the whole of the traditional doctrine of retribution overboard. Zophar's reaction is sharp and vicious: don't think that you can understand everything by your talk and chatter. It cannot be grasped at all, so submit to the traditional views and know that God's greatness is a divine mystery. When all the answers have been given, there is fortunately still always the divine mystery that no one knows except the one who refers to it. And so it is with Zophar. He will speak in the name of God and put Job's behaviour to shame. In contrast to Eliphaz, who regarded Job as innocent, and Bildad, who regarded the sons as guilty, Zophar now accuses Job outright of sin and calls on him to repent.

Zophar has had the good fortune to have been personally present at God's councils. Moreover he can spell out in detail how Job should have acted and how God has in fact treated Job better than he deserved. If Eliphaz makes a reference to the authority and knowledge that the friends themselves have and Bildad refers to the authority of the previous generations, Zophar appeals to no less than the authority of God himself. His approach is most common among believing comforters. They know that God's ways are unfathomable to anyone except themselves. It very soon proves that Zophar does not want to comfort at all, but to condemn Job's heresy. He would much have preferred God to accuse Job himself. He begins like this:

'Must such a multitude of words go unanswered,
and such a chatterbox be vindicated?
Must you reduce vulnerable people to silence,
so that you can mock without anyone shaming you,
and so that you can claim,
"My doctrine is pure, and I am clean in your eyes, O God"?
But oh, that God would himself speak,
and open his lips to you!
That he would tell you the secrets of wisdom,
for his works are mysterious.
Then you would be aware
that God still condones some of your sins' (11.2–8).

Zophar knows that if God had spoken he would have said the same thing as Zophar. He calls Job a chatterbox who claims to be innocent and in the meantime falsely accuses God. Charges like those that Job makes against God are foolish, says Zophar, since human beings do not understand anything of the divine mystery. 'What is blasphemy?', Zophar might prompt us to ask. Is it blasphemous to accuse God of dishonesty or injustice, even if that happens as a result of existential need? Isn't it far more blasphemous to behave as if you knew how God thinks, acts and feels, to behave as if you knew what offends God and what doesn't? Zophar calls accusing God blasphemous. Therefore he is quite certain that Job must swallow his words and stop this crazy talk in the future.

Job's ironic reaction

Job's answer is a long one. He doesn't seem to be aware that he is being accused of chattering on. His answer forms the conclusion to the whole discussion up to now. He begins in a more mocking and cynical way than ever:

'You are truly the voice of the people,
and wisdom will die with you.
But I have understanding as well as you;
I am not inferior to you.
Who does not know these things (that you say)?' (12.2–3).

He then immediately embarks on a mini-creation hymn:

> 'Ask the animals, and they will tell you,
> the birds of the air, and they will tell you.
> Or talk to the earth, and it will tell you,
> the fish of the sea, and they will tell you.
> Who among all of them does not know
> that the hand of YHWH has done this,
> in whose his hand is the life of every living being
> and the breath of every mortal?' (12.7–10).

What does Job mean by this poem in this ironical context? The poem can be read both as a hymn to creation and in precisely the opposite sense, namely as an ironic reference to the way in which the friends speak. In the first case it is to be regarded as a splendid creation poem in which the cosmic perspective completely replaces the anthropocentric perspective. Job then tells how the wild animals, the birds, the fishes and the earth form a living witness to their creator. They tell what human beings know, namely that YHWH has made everything. In the second case Job's poem is to be understood as irony, as an imitation of the simplistic way in which the friends speak against him. Just as the friends tell Job how simple the world is, so the animals and the plants tell them how simple the creation is. This emerges from the 'will tell you', which is repeated four times. The friends pretend that God's dealing with the world is simple, that it accords with logical principles and can even be understood by animals, fishes and plants. They regard the law of retribution as a natural law, a law by which life is lived. They promote the trite wisdom of these verses as deep insights. The rest of Job's account confirms this second, ironical reading of the poem, because in it Job cynically asks: 'Should old men be wise? Rivers wet? Judges competent? If it is up to God, he can do what he wants. Judges can become foolish, rivers dry and wise men incapable of understanding.' By this Job means that nothing is what it seems at first sight, that everything is much more complicated than the simple picture of creation and the traditional principle of retribution suggest.

Alongside this there is an element in the poem which indicates that it is not just meant in an ironical or mocking sense. It is striking that in this creation hymn Job uses the name YHWH. Elsewhere in the dialogues God is always denoted in a detached way with *elohim* or *eloah*, God or deity, and nowhere with the title, YHWH or Lord, with which believers address him. The word YHWH in this poem indicates that Job does not doubt the existence of YHWH and his creative power and that he therefore subscribes to the classical belief in creation. Like his friends, Job maintains the traditional belief that YHWH is the creator and lord of creation. On the other hand, the irony in his argument shows that he rejects the simplistic views of his friends and especially the connection that they take for granted between this belief in creation and their view of the order of creation. Job believes in YHWH as creator, but he thinks that you cannot understand everything simply by looking around you. In his view the law of retribution is not visible anywhere in creation. It is surely not the case that the good are always rewarded and the wicked are always punished. So it becomes clear that here, too, ambiguity in the text of Job has a function and refers to the double position which Job occupies. Without losing his faith in YHWH as creator, Job doubts the simple relationship between moral order and the created order as the friends expound it.

To illustrate the topicality of these problems and to show how even today people are automatically inclined to make a direct connection between the moral order and the order of creation, here are some quotations from an article by H. Versnel which appeared in the journal *Trouw* in December 1990.

During my most recent vacation I was appalled at the habits of Lanius Collurio. This attractive bird, commonly called the red-backed shrike, spends all day filling its larder. It catches beetles and spikes them on the thorns of a bush, carefully ensuring that the beetles remain alive and thus fresh. This living bramble took my breath away, since a key theological problem was struggling there . . . One cannot accuse the Bible of having excessive interest in or sympathy with animals, apart from a single lost sheep. But human beings suffer to no less a degree and that inevitably gives rise, both then and now, to the problem of the meaning of suffering and of theodicy (the question of the justice and justification of the divine order). The place where my red-

*backed shrike spiked its prey was by a lake. There I experienced
a tragedy which will dog me for the rest of my life. While
bathing, a girl got into deep water and her sister rushed to her
help. Both went under water. The first girl was found just in
time, but the second wasn't found until it was too late. Talking
to a Greek woman about this tragedy I asked her how she could
reconcile this with her faith. She had three answers which she
gave quickly one after another. I could choose. It was a punishment from God. Or it was written (had been predestined). Or
God takes those who love him when they are young. She had an
answer to everything. Of course you will recognize this
approach, as we find it particularly in our Dutch churches; it is
rather more thickly sown on the higher dunes and in the heavy
clay. Predestination, punishment, testing, one can still meet the
whole sadistic universe there in the wild. But recently a new
antiphon has been heard to these 'answers to evil', deeply
rooted in the firm ground of centuries. If creation indeed houses
so many paradoxical, structural and biologically necessary
atrocities, God cannot have created the world. Not only can
God not have created it in six days; God cannot have created it
at all, certainly not like that.*

Versnel offers his readers the following choice: either the order
of creation needs to run in accordance with the law of retribution or there is no order of creation at all. Now the existence of
a red-backed shrike and its prey, and the fact that a girl is
drowned and her sister is saved, themselves prove that the order
of creation does not run in accordance with the (human) laws of
justice. The Greek woman whom he cites talks like Job's
friends, and she defends the first solution. In her view the order
of creation and thus the events in the lake which were described
take place in accordance with the principle of retribution. The
author rejects this and asks whether we would not do better to
conclude that there is no order of creation. He thus opts for the
second solution. However, Job's poem and the whole book of
Job show that the order of creation is one thing and retribution
another. YHWH as creator and the creation are to be evaluated
separately, and the human moral order is not to be regarded as
a guiding principle of the order of creation.

After Job has both recognized the creative power of YHWH

and brought out the simplistic attitude of his friends in the first
part of his argument (12.1–12), in the second part he attacks the
capriciousness with which God exercises his power:

'With him are wisdom and might,
from him are counsel and understanding . . .
If he withholds the waters, there is drought;
if he sends them out, they flood the land . . .
He leads counsellors away stripped,
and judges he makes fools . . .
He deprives of speech those who are trusted,
and takes away the discernment of the elders . . .
He reveals the mysteries of darkness
and brings deep darkness to light.
He raises up nations and he destroys them . . .
He bewilders the understanding of the leaders of the people,
and makes them wander in a pathless waste.
They grope in the dark without light;
he makes them stagger like drunkards' (12.13–25).

God may be both the creator and powerful governor of the universe, but he misuses his power. Job fiercely opposed the sheer
caprice with which God seems to use his authority. He criticizes
this behaviour of God's. What is one to do with a God who is so
untrustworthy? Job is tossed to and fro between faith and
abhorrence. He apparently agrees with Zophar when he says
that God is indeed wise, but he undermines Zophar's account
by emphasizing God's capriciousness. Job's doubt is becoming
increasingly clear, and he finds it increasingly difficult to combine the traditional truths of faith with his experiences.
However, sometimes he expresses his criticism and despair
ironically to make it tolerable.

Job is not content with explanations from above. Moreover
in the end he abandons the cosmic approach and takes his own
experience as a starting point. He says as a rebuke to Zophar:

'Listen rather to my reasoning,
hear the accusations of my lips.
Is it for God's honour that you speak falsely?
Is it for him that you lie?

Will you show partiality towards him,
and play God's advocate?' (13.6–8)

Job calls on Zophar and his other friends to be open to him and
really listen to him. They must not only argue on the basis of
their faith but look reality in the face and listen to him, Job. He
is also speaking from his experience. Then Job's problem again
becomes evident. On the one hand he rebukes his friends for
not starting from experience of God but from doctrine. On the
other hand this causes him problems because he cannot reconcile his experience with this same doctrine. He has not yet
thrown the doctrine overboard and continues to hold on to it.
His charge that God is unjust, even cruel, derives from the fact
that he, too, wants there to be a rational explanation for everything that takes place in the world. He, too, wants God's action
to be an adequate reaction to human reaction. Thus up to this
movement Job continues to think that human suffering does not
happen by chance but comes from God, and he continues to
make a direct connection between God and the world. In fact
this is the same application of rational or logical principles to
God. However, in the eyes of the friends God acts in a good,
albeit perhaps sometimes incomprehensible, way, while according to Job he acts in a bad and arbitrary way.

Job's fate grips us. We share it, and we share his perspective.
Moreover we sympathize with Job's sombre musings at the end
of the first round of conversations when he says, 'I asked God
for justice, I asked God for compassion, but God only showed
me his most inhuman face. I loved God in a truly disinterested
way, but God does not even respect this unselfish love.' Job's
hope seems to have fled, for where can he turn now that the
traditional views of God's justice prove to be false? Job no
longer feels inclined to discuss with his friends. The only thing
that he still wants is for God himself to speak. He wants to present his case (13.18) and says: 'Let's fight it out, putting traditional wisdom and my experience side by side; then let's see
what you, God, have to say to that.' From this challenge it
proves that Job has not yet given up completely. Evidently he
has not yet bowed his head. The bell for the end of the first
round has gone. Job has been hit hard, but he will fight on.

The Second Round of Conversation: Job 15–21

The long first series of conversations between Job and his friends is followed by a shorter second and an even shorter third round. The familiar standpoints recur. Everyone wants to win everyone else over to his own position. Therefore it is possible to report the second and third rounds rather more briefly.

Eliphaz

Eliphaz begins to talk. What he says can be read in two ways, just like the first dialogue between him and Job. If Eliphaz had spoken so ambiguously only the first time, that could be by chance. But now that he also speaks like this the second time round, we can say that this ambivalence is characteristic of him. Eliphaz says that Job does not speak as a wise man and criticizes him for letting his tongue run away with him. If Job had been truly wise, then he would have known that no one, not even angels, can be completely innocent. So it is impossible for him to be completely innocent and therefore he can expect a certain degree of suffering. Eliphaz continues to assert that Job is not bad, and this is the positive side of his message. But he does portray the fate of wicked people at length. It is as if Eliphaz wants to say that this is the fate that Job can also expect. If he continues to behave like this, he is calling down this misery upon himself.

Eliphaz depicts very vividly the disastrous fate that the godless can expect. Because the evildoers and the godless have challenged God by their evil way of living, they know that God will exact retribution for their evil deeds. Eliphaz compares the godless with a warrior fighting against God (15.25–27). He goes on the offensive and assaults God, protecting himself behind his shield. But what a poor warrior he is! He is in bad shape, because he has not been trained properly and he is too fat. Will such a fat man attack God and keep up the fight? It can only end in disaster. Eliphaz's mocking description is certainly witty. Like this warrior, Job is fighting with God, but it is hard to compare him with such a foolish and fat warrior. Job will hardly be very fat after his long stay on the heap of ashes. Moreover Eliphaz does not make any direct connection here between Job and the godless, though he is playful and mocking enough. He teases Job with a view to making him repent. By comparisons and twists in his argument Eliphaz tries to make Job change his behaviour.

Eliphaz still does not regard Job as guilty, but asks what is up with him. How can Job speak like this? It seems as if he has turned against God (15.13). The verb 'turn' that Eliphaz uses here has two meanings. In this case Eliphaz is also indicating that Job is turning away from God, whereas normally this verb denotes 'conversion', i.e. turning towards God. Eliphaz thinks that Job has turned away from God and wants Job to turn to God. To achieve this Eliphaz pesters Job with every means at his disposal, from good will and conviction to irony and mockery.

As well as the mockery and irony, Eliphaz's argument has a strong negative tone, which is produced by the serious accusations that he makes against Job. He calls Job's standpoint sheer heresy and says that the doctrine of God that Job has just developed is an insult to any pious person. This heresy even makes any piety impossible, because retribution disappears as the basic principle. In that case there can be no further justification, no fair distribution of happiness and unhappiness on the basis of good or evil deeds.

'You are doing away with fear (of God)
and diminishing reverence before God's face' (15.4).

In the prologue Job is called 'godfearing', first by the narrator and later by God himself. Eliphaz has also praised his friend as godfearing in his first speech (4.6). Clearly something has changed, since Eliphaz is now accusing Job of having violated this fear of God. That is a serious accusation. The term 'fear (of God)' denotes the proper and fundamental attitude which a

believer adopts towards God; according to Eliphaz, as a result
of Job and his chattering there is a risk that this fear will be
replaced by an anxiety before God like that felt by the sinner
aware of his guilt. For if a good believer feels only anxiety and
anxiously has to await the arbitrary choice that God will make,
what basis is there still for a relationship between believer and
God? The moment that the traditional doctrine of moral
retribution is thrown overboard, there is no longer any ground
for faith. Godless and believers alike then both feel the same
sort of anxiety about God. Eliphaz seems to be the first to see
what it means for the doctrine of retribution to be thrown overboard. If it is, the whole of belief in God must be revised, since
it can no longer be based on reward for good action or punishment for bad action, and Eliphaz cannot have that. Despite his
vision he holds firm to his 'orthodox' belief. This tells him what
fear of God looks like and what is the right way to act. In the
following old Jewish story (in a version by Nico ter Linden) the
scribe can be compared with the orthodox believer Eliphaz,
who is sure of his knowledge.

The story of the young shepherd boy

*There was once a young shepherd boy who was unable to say
the Hebrew prayers. The only thing that he did was to say every
day, 'Lord of the world, you know that if you had cattle and
gave them to me to look after – from everyone else I ask payment for looking after their cattle – for you I would do it for
nothing, because I love you.' One day a scribe came by and
heard the shepherd saying his prayer, 'Lord of the world, you
know that if you had cattle.' 'Fool,' said this scribe, 'you
mustn't pray like that.' 'How must I pray, then?' asked the
shepherd. The scribe taught him the benedictions in the right
order, the* shema *and silent prayer. 'Now you can pray the right
way,' said the scribe. But after he had gone away the shepherd
forgot all that he had learned and stopped praying. He no
longer dared to pray his former prayer because the scribe had
forbidden that. One night the scribe had a dream. A voice said,
'Unless you tell the shepherd boy that he may pray again as he
used to do, you will meet with a great misfortune. For you have*

robbed me of one of my most valuable sons.' Next morning the scribe went back to the shepherd boy. *'What do you pray?'* 'I don't pray at all,' replied the shepherd boy, 'because I couldn't remember what you taught me and you had forbidden me to pray *"If you had cattle."'* Then the scribe told him what he had dreamed. *'Now I know that what I said was not good. Please go on praying as you used to.'*

Job's reaction to Eliphaz

Job reacts to Eliphaz in immediately understandable language: 'I've often heard such things, you miserable comforters. If I speak, my suffering doesn't disappear, and if I am silent it does not leave me either. So what must I do?' Job complains to his friends and insists that they should feel what he feels. There is indeed a great difference between having to suffer oneself and seeing someone else suffering. Job thinks that his friends would show more compassion if they were to experience what he is enduring. This is the nub of the problem of sympathy: real sympathy like that of Job's friends is difficult, because you don't feel what the other is feeling. The friends haven't lost their children, don't suffer from a skin infection, haven't lost their possessions . . . But surely one can hardly rebuke them for that? This rebuke of Job's doesn't seem at all fair. Certainly he is right when he says, 'Would you prefer me to keep my mouth shut and say nothing more, and my silence to devour me from within?' Nothing is changed, whether he goes on speaking or remains silent. In that case speaking is better, although the friends get a whole load of complaints.

Because the friends don't understand, Job begins by accusing God and says, 'Formerly all went well with me. I was in harmony with myself, with my family and the world around. Now I'm a broken man. There is no longer a line in my life. You, God, follow me like a warrior and your arrows fly around me. You ram me open, breach after breach, and storm after me like a warrior' (16.13–14). Job takes up the imagery used by Eliphaz: not he but God is the attacker. Now Job accuses God not only of capriciousness but also of cruelty:

'He has now broken me completely.
You have destroyed my circle of friends.
You have shrivelled me up, that is my witness,
my leanness accuses me.
He has torn me in his wrath,
he has gnashed his teeth at me;
my adversary lowers at me with his eyes' (16.7–9).

God as Job experiences him is harsh and cruel. Here Job applies existing lamentations against enemies which often occur in the Psalms to God himself: the images of God and the enemy fuse together. That explains the strange alternation between the third person (he) and the second person (you). The attack on God takes the form of a lamentation against the enemies, in which God and the enemies increasingly coincide. Nowhere else in biblical literature is such an image of God as the enemy of humankind to be found, and this strong formulation accentuates Job's despair:

'My spirit is broken,
my days are extinct,
and only the grave remains for me' (17.1).

But Job's resilience quickly asserts itself and he goes over to the counter-attack against his friends. He calls them mockers, and indeed Eliphaz was very mocking. But Job can do the same thing. He accuses his friends of merely being parrots, who repeat one another and the tradition. So look what your friends are good for, only as a source of offence to keep your spirit alive!

'My eyes have grown dim from grief,
and all my members are like a shadow.
Upright men are appalled at this,
and the innocent stirs himself up against the godless.
Yet the righteous holds fast to his way,
and he that has clean hands grows stronger and stronger.
But all of you, come back, come back,
I cannot find a wise man among you' (17.7–10).

Job is in the right and his friends must change. Job returns once more to the image that Eliphaz used: not he but they must change. Job's conviction that he is innocent remains. His self-confidence has increased. He is the righteous one who is in opposition and, as we literally read, 'increases in strength'.

After this flickering up of his self-confidence, Job sinks back again: my days are past, my plans have failed. But even in this hopeless phase there is a mocking and a questioning search. This is again evident from the last sentences of his reaction to Eliphaz (17.14–15):

> 'If I call to the grave, "You are my father,"
> and to the worms, "My mother," "My sister,"
> Where then is my hope?
> Who can discover my hope?'

Bildad and Job

After this Bildad speaks. In his first speech he urged Job to learn from the disaster that overcame his children. In his second speech he confronts Job with the fate that the evil or godless meet with. Job could meet with this same fate, although Bildad of course hopes that he will repent in time to escape such a disaster. Bildad sketches out almost passionately, in a coherent argument, the disasters which overtake an evil man. Such a man gets entangled in his own net of words and deeds, so that it becomes clear that wickedness punishes itself. As if that were not evidence of the order which exists in the world! Bildad thus depicts in vivid images the traditional theology of cause and effect, of action and consequence, but applies them only to the wicked. He ends his argument like this (18.18–21):

> 'He is thrust from light into darkness
> and driven out of the world.
> He has no offspring or descendant among his people,
> and no survivor in his house.
> The west is appalled at his fate,
> the east is seized with horror.
> Surely such are the dwellings of the ungodly,
> this is the place of him who does not know God.'

The 'he' of whom Bildad speaks is the godless. At the same time he puts Job on the same level as this godless person, for Job no longer has any children, so that his descendants have vanished from the earth. In the east and the west people are appalled at the fate that Job has met with. There can only be one cause for all this, namely that Job has sinned and thus brought this misery upon himself.

Job reacts in fury. 'How long will you torment my soul and smash me with words? You have insulted me at least ten times, you are not ashamed to humiliate me' (19.2–3). Job sees how his friends leave him in the lurch. They prefer to accuse him of injustice rather than give up their idea of a righteous God. Job says that it does not even make sense to refer to God any more, since God too has become his enemy. Everyone – God, family, friends and servants – has abandoned him. Job even mentions his wife in this connection: 'I am repulsive to my wife' (19.17). Already in the prologue Job felt misunderstood by his wife, and now he feels how his whole body appals her. Instead of attracting her, he puts her off like someone with foul breath. Job is aware of his own repulsiveness. He is a bag of bones and filthy all over, and you can smell him a mile off. No one, not even his servants, still honours or respects him. In fact his close friends, with whom he is in conversation here, have stopped listening to him. But he makes one more attempt:

> 'Have pity on me, have pity on me
> you my friends,
> for the hand of God has touched me!
> Why do you, like God, pursue me?
> Why are you not satisfied with my flesh?' (19.21–22).

Although he no longer believes in it, he makes one last appeal to someone (19.23–27). He calls this person a *goel*, a redeemer. *Goel*, a legal term, is the member of a family who frees you from a desperate situation. He is someone who avenges a murdered member of the family, or who buys back family land which was sold for debts or because of the death of its owner, or who redeems a member of the family who has been sold as a slave. So what would this *goel* have to do for Job? In fact he is the last source of help or appeal still left for Job, the last person who can restore him. Who can take on the role of redeemer or mediator for Job? The members of his family are dead, and his children are no more. Women are not thought capable of taking on the role of redeemer. Is there still someone who could fulfil this function? Alas, Job knows all too well that the answer to his question must be in the negative: for him there is no last means of redemption, no *goel*. Had it been otherwise, then Job himself would have turned to this redeemer. However, it seems that simply by putting the question of a redeemer, Job still shows a flicker of hope. Then even this spark of hope disappears and Job has to let go even of this last straw. There is no one else he can ask for redemption or help; no one can still provide it for him. So his call for a *goel* is not to be seen as a hopeful expression, but more as a last sigh which underlies the hopelessness of his position. It is a sharp expression of pain caused by a vindictive and angry God. No one can mediate between Job and this God.

Zophar and Job

Zophar acknowledges that he is shocked by Job's words and describes at even greater length than Bildad the fate of the wicked or godless, in order still to protect Job from this fate. He tells Job how briefly the godless can enjoy the fruits of their evil deeds. Although they think that they have achieved something, their joy is transitory.

> 'Do you not know this from of old,
> since man was placed upon earth,
> that the exulting of the wicked is short,
> and the joy of the godless but for a moment?
> Though his pride mounts up to heaven
> and his head reaches to the clouds,
> he passes away for ever like his own dung' (20.4–7a).

As a result of the self-destructive power of sin, bad behaviour is not punished by something or someone from outside; destruction comes above all from within. Quite suddenly an end can come to the life of the godless. His life can fly away like a dream. The basis of Zophar's speech is of course the traditional doctrine of retribution, according to which the godless will feel the consequences of their actions. In his first round Zophar asserted that Job's suffering showed that he was a sinner; in this second round he develops this and its consequences for Job. Job will suffer the fate of the godless, unless he listens to Zophar's plea to him to repent.

In answer to Zophar Job asks two questions. Why do good men prosper? How often do they fail in their evil enterprises?

> 'Why do the wicked go on living,
> reach old age, and increase in power?
> Their children are established in their presence,
> and their offspring before their eyes.
> Their houses are safe from fear,
> and no rod of God is upon them' (21.7–9).

Over against Zophar's assertion that the godless only achieve short-term success and have a short life, Job sets his own experience that they do have success and live to old age. Earlier Eliphaz had spoken about the fear of God which in the godless turns to anxiety. Job thinks that they do not feel any anxiety at all. People who do not fear God get what they want; people who do fear God, like Job, don't. Death comes to them all, however they have lived. One dies bitterly and another peacefully, but everyone, godfearer or godless, goes to Sheol, where the worms eat them up.

Job judges by what he sees around him. His experience teaches him that things go well with the godless. According to him, that is a fact. Zophar's argument is a simple repetition of what in the tradition is called justice, but according to Job this is blind to the facts. God's reliability cannot be proved, either through experience or argument, since God does not give any certain recompense or retribution in this life. The godless ignore God, yet God rewards them. It is striking that the description of the lot of the godless is very like the traditional picture of the righteous. But in Job's view the roles are not simply exchanged. It is not that the righteous suffer and the wicked prosper. What Job means is that a person can have no confidence that the just will be rewarded and the unjust punished. Job can no longer believe the clear theories of the tradition, since life shows another pattern.

At the end of the first round of conversation Job had asked his friends to be silent and listen to him. That would comfort him more than all the talk. What did they do? They began a second round of conversation. At the beginning and the end of his reaction to Zophar Job asks again whether they will listen to him instead of accusing him and mocking him. He ends the second round with the question, 'Why do you give me nothing but idle comfort? Your answers are nothing but deceit.'

The Third Round of Conversation: Job 22–27

Despite Job's request for silence, for a healthy silence, the friends again react with talk, though they do not expect to be able to convince Job. But you never know your luck. However, there is no progress in this conversation and it seems more like a kind of repetition. Everyone repeats his standpoint, but does so in a rather more extreme way. That is true above all of Eliphaz, who reacts at the greatest length, though he has already lost heart. Bildad reacts very briefly and Zophar does not say anything more at all. Even Job has lost the thread somewhat. His reaction to Eliphaz is long and more confused than before, and his retort to Bildad is more sarcastic than we are accustomed to.

Eliphaz again produces stories of God's omnipotence and the impotence of human beings. He gives a list of ethically responsible actions which looks rather like a traditional standard list from an introductory book on normative ethics. Job has evidently failed to perform the actions which are summarized here and therefore deserves his misery. Eliphaz does not know from his own experience that Job has made mistakes, but has to deduce it from the misery that now befalls Job. At long last he once again calls on Job to repent and make his peace with God.

The despair which Job feels, now that he can no longer share the insights which have been handed down in faith, is tangible in his reaction to Eliphaz. What is he still to believe, how is he to go on living, if everything that he experiences does not match the tradition of faith in which he too used to believe, and if God has become increasingly independent of accepted dogmas? What is to be done if the God whom he has summoned to court in a kind of summary process does not appear? Then chaos breaks in, as is evident from Job's answer to Eliphaz:

'Oh, that I knew where I might find him,
that I might come even to his abode!
Then I would lay my case before him
and fill my mouth with arguments . . .
No, he would give heed to me.
Then an upright man could reason with him
and I should be acquitted for ever by my judge.
Behold, I go to the east, but he is not there;
to the west, but I cannot perceive him;
if he is at work in the north I do not discover him;
if he turns to the south I do not see him' (23.3–9).

So God cannot be found. God knows the way of human beings, but human beings do not know the way of God. After speaking of his own case, Job goes on to speak of the problems of injustice generally. That is very strange when we remember that Job is accusing his friends of beginning not from concrete experience but from theory. And now, like his friends, he is speaking in general terms, about criminals and evildoers and the fate that they all meet with. Job seems to be generalizing, and mixing a lot of things up.

Then Bildad speaks for the last time in the form of a song of praise, in which he celebrates the greatness of God, and the littleness of human beings.

'How then can a man be righteous before God?
How can he who is born of woman be clean?
Behold, even the moon is not bright
and the stars are not pure in his sight.
How much less man, who is a maggot,
and the son of man, who is a worm?' (25.4–6).

Bildad is so short of material that it seems as if Job has interrupted him. Job's reaction is aggressive and sarcastic, 'What help have you given me with all your wise advice?', and he immediately composes his own hymn to the negative sides of God's omnipotence (26.5–14). Perhaps Job pauses in expectation of a reaction from Zophar. But Zophar does not say anything else and has lost heart. Reaction or not, Job goes further. He bursts out into a lament against God. But even then Job has not really given up the struggle:

'As God lives, who has taken away my right,
and the Almighty, who has made my soul bitter;
as long as my breath is in me,
and the spirit of God is in my nostrils,
my lips will not speak falsehood,
and my tongue will not utter deceit.
I hold fast my righteousness, and will not let it go' (27.2–6).

A splendid, defensive end to a long, very long, dialogue.

Job's Second Monologue: Job 28–31

1. There is a mine for silver,
   and a place where they wash out gold.
2. Iron is taken out of the earth
   and copper is smelted from the stone.
3. Men put an end to darkness
   and search out to the farthest bound
   the ore in deepest darkness.
4. They bore mine-shafts far from where people live;
   they hang with no support for their feet,
   they toil far away from people.
5. The earth from which comes forth bread
   underneath is stirred up as by fire.
6. Its stones are the place where sapphires are discovered,
   and it also has gold dust.
7. The path there no bird of prey knows,
   and the falcon's eye has not seen it.
8. The proud beasts have not trodden it;
   the lion has not passed over it.
9. Man puts his hand to the flinty rock
   and overturns mountains by the roots.
10. He bores channels in the rocks,
    and his eye discovers every precious thing.
11. He dams the sources of the rivers,
    and the hidden treasures he brings to light.
12. But where can wisdom be found?
    Where is the place of understanding?

13. No man knows her value,
    she cannot be found in the land of the living.
14. The deep says, 'She is not in me,'
    the sea says, 'She is not with me.'
15. She cannot be bought for gold,
    silver cannot be paid as her price.
16. She cannot be valued in the finest gold of Ophir,

in precious onyx or sapphire.

17. Gold and glass cannot equal her in value
 nor can she be exchanged for jewels of fine gold.

18. Coral and crystal cannot be mentioned in the same breath;
 the price of wisdom is above pearls.

19. Topaz from Cush cannot compare with her value,
 nor can she be valued in pure gold.

20. But where does wisdom come from?
 Where is the place of understanding?

21. She is removed from the eyes of all that lives,
 it is hidden even from the birds of the air.

22. Destruction and death say,
 'We have heard a rumour of her with our ears.'

23. God has insight into the way to her,
 he knows her place.

24. For his gaze extends to the ends of the earth,
 he sees everything under the heavens.

25. When he gave to the wind its weight,
 and meted out the waters by measure,

26. when he made a decree for the rain
 and a way for the thunderclouds,

27. then he saw her and declared her;
 he established her and searched her out.

28. To man he said,
 'Behold, the fear of the Lord is wisdom;
 and to keep far from evil is understanding.'

1. Job continued his argument and said:

2. 'Oh, that I were as in the months of old,
 as in the days when God watched over me;

3. when his lamp shone above my head,
 and by his light I walked through the darkness;

4. as I was in the prime of my life,
 when the friendship of God protected my tent from above,

5. when the Almighty was yet with me,
 and my children were round about me;

6. when my feet were washed with milk,
 and the rocks poured out streams of oil for me.

7. When I went out to the gate of the city
 and prepared my seat in the square,

8. the young men saw me and withdrew,
 and the aged rose and stood;

9. the men of note refrained from talking,
   and laid their hand on their mouth;
10. the voice of the leaders was hushed,
    and their tongue cleaved to the roof of their mouth.
11. The ear that heard called me blessed,
    the eye that saw me approved.
23. They waited for me as for the rain;
    and opened their mouths wide as for the spring rain.
24. I smiled on them, they could not believe it;
    the light of my countenance they did not cast down.
25. I chose their way and sat as chief,
    I dwelt like a king in the midst of an army,
    like one who comforts mourners.

1. But now they make sport of me, they who are younger than I,
   whose fathers I would have disdained to set with my shepherds'
   dogs.
9. But now I have become their mocking song,
   I am a byword to them.
10. They abhor me and they keep aloof from me;
    they do not hesitate to spit at the sight of me.
15. Terrors are turned upon me;
    my honour is swept away as by the wind,
    and my prosperity has passed away like a cloud.
16. But now life is flowing away from me;
    days of misery hold of me in their grip.
17. The night racks my bones,
    and the pain that gnaws me takes no rest.
18. With great force it seizes my garment;
    it grips me by the collar of my tunic.
19. He has cast me into the mire,
    and I have become like dust and ashes.
20. I call to you for help, but you do not answer me;
    I stand there, but you do not heed me.
21. You have become my tyrant,
    and your mighty hand persecutes me.
22. You lift me up and make me ride on the wind,
    and toss me to and fro in the storm.
23. I know that you will drive me back to death,
    and to the house appointed for all living.

The two parts of the monologue

After the long discussion between Job and his friends, in chapter 28 there follows a well-composed and attractive poem in which Job celebrates wisdom. It is quite different in tone from the previous chapters, in which soberness dominates. This poem is markedly positive and is a true hymn of praise to wisdom. It is striking that immediately after it, in chapters 29–31, Job again bursts out into a lament and passionately asserts his innocence. How does all this fit together? What is the connection between these chapters?

A usual answer to this question is that the hymn to wisdom in chapter 28 is part of the dialogue, whereas chapters 29–31 form an independent monologue by Job. In the hymn then Job opposes the traditional standpoint of his friends: 'You think that you have a monopoly of wisdom, but that is wrong, because only God possesses wisdom.' This view certainly corresponds with the preceding text, but the relationship with chapters 29–31 then remains unclear. For if Job in chapter 28 thinks that he cannot find wisdom, why does he protest so loudly in chapters 29–31? Wouldn't it have been more honest for him to persist in his wretchedness and ignorance?

Quite a different solution to this question is that chapter 28 and chapters 29–31 are both part of Job's monologue. I prefer this view. In chapter 28, the hymn of praise to wisdom, Job is addressing no one in particular, neither his friends not God. Nor is Job speaking to anyone other than himself in chapters 29–31. Both form a long monologue and they have a definite relationship to each other. In the first part Job gives a positive picture of wisdom in an all-seeing perspective from 'above'. In the second part he shows a negative picture, the other side of the coin, namely the perspective from 'below', or concrete life here and now. These two perspectives are in counterpoint. They form the voice and counter-voice in a poetic monologue (or an internal dialogue) by Job.

The structure of the book of Job then proves to have been thought out very carefully. Just as Job's first monologue in chapter 3 functions as a hinge between the prologue and the dialogues, so Job's second monologue in chapters 28–31 makes possible the transition from the dialogue to the last part of the book. In this second monologue, Job's hymn about wisdom in chapter 28 points forward to the rest of the book and especially to God's speech, and Job's assertion of his innocence in chapters 29–31 points back to the previous dialogues in the book. Together the two parts of this monologue then form the second hinge or turning-point in the book. The book of Job resembles a triptych even more strongly than we have already seen. The 'prologue', 'dialogue' and 'theologue' (speech of God) are so to speak the three panels connected by Job's two monologues, which form the hinges.

Part one: the hymn to wisdom

The first part of Job's monologue in chapter 28 is a carefully worked-out poem; its structure is clear and it communicates directly through splendid imagery. The equilibrium of wisdom is reflected by the equilibrium of the text. The structure of the poem indicates three strophes of approximately equal length, each of which is concluded by a pithy refrain:

'But where does wisdom come from?
Where is the place of understanding?' (28.12, 20).

In the first strophe of his hymn of praise Job celebrates human power and impotence:

'There is a mine for silver,
and a place where they wash out gold.
Iron is taken out of the earth
and copper is smelted from stone.
Men put an end to darkness
and search out to the farthest bound
the ore in deepest darkness.
Man puts his hand to the flinty rock
and overturns mountains by the roots.
He bores channels in the rocks,
and his eye discovers every precious thing.
He dams the sources of the rivers,
and the hidden treasures he brings to light.
But where can wisdom be found?
Where is the place of understanding?' (28.1–12)

This is a description of the actions which human beings perform with pride and wonder. They even master this technique of mining! Human beings are capable of this seeking and discovering, smelting iron ore and polishing precious stones, extracting what is hidden! They investigate the depths of the earth and the breadth of the horizon, but nevertheless they do not find wisdom. Thus there is no question of the bankruptcy of human skill, or even of scepticism about human worth. The human drive to investigate is seen in a positive light. Among other things, this is evident from the word *chaqar*, investigate, which within this one poem expresses the positive worth both of human beings (28.3) and of God (28.27). However, there are clear limitations. Human beings, who are capable of so much, are not capable of finding wisdom; their worth is limited by contrast with that of God.

It emerges from the second strophe that wisdom, which cannot be found, cannot be purchased either. Gold and silver cannot function as a price of wisdom. Even topaz from Cush or Egypt, i.e. topaz of the highest quality, is not valuable enough to be exchanged for wisdom. The value of wisdom is higher than anything. The term 'value' occurs three times in the second strophe, and each time there is a negative with it. At all events, human beings do not know the value of wisdom. After the first strophe has mentioned and praised all human skills, the second strophe puts all the emphasis on the inability of human beings to gain wisdom. All creatures fall short here. Even the phenomena which already existed before creation, like the depths and the (primal) ocean, do not know how to find wisdom:

> 'The deep says, "She is not in me,"
> the sea says, "She is not with me" ' (28.14).

Wisdom cannot be found, nor dug up, nor exchanged for precious metal or money. Human beings cannot experience her with their senses. God is the only one who knows the way to wisdom and who has found her.

> 'God has insight into the way to her,
> he knows her place.
> For his gaze extends to the ends of the earth,
> he sees everything under the heavens.

When he gave to the wind its weight,
and meted out the waters by measure,
when he made a decree for the rain
and a way for the thunderclouds,
then he saw her and declared her;
he established her and searched her out.
To man he said,
"Behold, the fear of the Lord is wisdom;
and to keep far from evil is understanding"' (28.23–28).

When God was planning and establishing the cosmos, he discovered wisdom. So wisdom is a phenomenon which precedes creation and at the same time is revealed through and to God in the process of creation itself. Wisdom is the ordering principle of his process of creation, the hidden design behind everything. God is the only one who has seen wisdom, but where has he seen her? Not in the deepest depths, nor in the greatest heights; not at the ends of the earth, but in the totality of creation. For human beings who are part of this creation, wisdom is a bit too great. Wisdom is invisible to the human eye and too complicated to be discerned by the human spirit and to be 'sought out'. So human beings must be content with a kind of derived wisdom:

'Wisdom is the fear of the Lord ;
and to keep far from evil is understanding' (28.28).

Human beings cannot acquire wisdom, but only attain to her indirectly by way of the creation and the creator. Second-hand knowledge, the peak of insight that human beings can acquire, can only achieve this through the 'first owner' or originator. By recognizing and respecting him as lord of creation and by refraining from bad behaviour, human beings can achieve an appropriate degree of wisdom.

Job has lived in accordance with this insight. The prologue describes how he has feared God and refrained from evil. God also recognizes this. Nevertheless, much misery has come upon Job. But he has continued to live by this 'wisdom', even after all that he has experienced. In the dialogues Job has asked for an account and demanded an explanation. In this second monologue, in the song of praise to wisdom (Job 28), he once again formulates his view of wisdom and then in chapters 29–31 protests once again: 'I have in fact lived in accordance with these insights and I have feared God and refrained from evil. I am innocent, this misery dishonours me.' And he demands that God should behave in a different way.

Part two: past, present and future

In contrast to the ideal picture of wisdom in the first part of his monologue, in the second part Job presents his actual life of misery. He recalls his happy past (chapter 29), compares it with his sorry present in the form of a lament (chapter 30), and finally tries by means of a confession of innocence to get a view of his future (chapter 31). The confession takes the form of an oath: 'If I have acted wickedly, then let me be punished'; 'If I have done evil, let me be punished like this.' This series of oaths must in his view inevitably lead to the conclusion, 'I have not done this or that evil, and so I must be restored to my old state.' In this way Job tries to sketch out a particular future which is better than his present sorry situation. This part of Job's monologue thus proves to have been constructed in just as balanced a way as the first part. The three strophes relating to past, present and future can together be heard as the second voice in a duet with the first voice of the hymn to wisdom.

The good old days

'Oh, that I were as in the months of old,
as in the days when God watched over me;
when his lamp shone above my head,
and by his light I walked through the darkness;
as I was in the prime of my life,
when the friendship of God protected my tent from above,
when the Almighty was yet with me,
and my children were round about me . . .
When I went out to the gate of the city
and prepared my seat in the square,
the young men saw me and withdrew,
and the aged rose and stood;

the men of note refrained from talking,
and laid their hand on their mouth;
the voice of the leaders was hushed,
and their tongue cleaved to the roof of their mouth.
The ear that heard called me blessed,
the eye that saw me approved' (29.2–11).

Job sighs, 'Once God protected me and all went well with me. Then God was not a gaoler and a spy but a companion and a protector.' In the past he was the greatest, richest and most honoured person in the city. Now he thinks, 'Everyone respected me then and I intended the best for everyone.' And at that time he thought that this would always be the case.

However, Job's sigh can also be read in quite a different way. Above all the last part of the chapter suggests this:

'They waited for me as for the rain;
and opened their mouths wide as for the spring rain.
I smiled on them, they could not believe it;
the light of my countenance they did not cast down.
I chose their way and sat as chief,
I dwelt like a king in the midst of an army, like one who comforts mourners' (29.23–25).

Here Job describes himself as an ideal prince and ruler. He does not emphasize the great and mighty deeds which God has done but his own greatness, importance and prestige. In his recollections of the past God was his protector (29.4–5), but the other great deeds were due to Job himself. God is not mentioned again after v.5. We recognize something familiar in Job's behaviour: everything that human beings have done well they have done themselves, and all the injustice that has come upon them stems from God. This is like parents who say that the good in their children is due to them and attribute the bad in their children to outside influences,

It is striking that in his praise of himself Job uses expressions which are usually reserved for God. Thus Job mentions 'the light of his countenance' as the source of blessing for others, whereas normally only 'the light of God's countenance' is said to bring blessing. It is apt that Job says that he chose the way or the direction of the people who fell under his control. Because his authority over them was absolute, he decided where they went or did not go. Job was the boss and his will was law. Really only God is said to choose the way and the direction of human beings; only God is said to be the absolute ruler under whose government everything falls. God will refer to this statement of Job's later, in his speech from the storm. There he challenges Job: 'Job, you are such a good leader, govern the cosmos if you can and distribute justice over all the world. Then I too will praise you and celebrate you' (40.14).

Job looks at his past through rose-coloured spectacles. Everything then was utterly good, in contrast to today, when everything is utterly bad. And of course the future once again has to be like the past. However understandable Job's reflections on the past may be, they show his limited view. Everything is good when he is the one who has power over other people and when he is the only person. This 'just' ordering of society in which Job was the leader has been lost. The shortcomings of Job's imagery are clear. Everyone prefers to see himself in the position of the rich and powerful, but now to act as though that constitutes a just and righteous human society and to demand of God that he restore such an unequal distribution of power, at least when the power again falls to Job, is something else. So Job's allusions are ambivalent. They are understandable as a sigh over his loss, but at the same time they show their limitations.

The sorry past

The tone of Job's lament which immediately follows differs notably from the powerful tone that we have just heard. There is no longer a proud parade of a famous past. The opening sentence, 'but now', emphasizes the marked antithesis between Job's former status of ideal ruler and his lowly position now. Three times this harsh contrast between past and present is repeated: 'but now' he is laughed at and mocked; 'but now' they attack him like warriors; 'but now' he is only dust and ashes, and death is near. All honour, respect and authority has gone. So too has life and prosperity, and death is all that remains to him.

In 30.2–11 Job describes his lot as that of an outcast. Hidden in caves, the outcasts live like wild animals outside the city, excluded by everyone. They are regarded as inhuman, as nameless figures who have lost their function in society. It then proves that Job has become the outcast of these outcasts. Even these creatures laugh at him. The one whose face gave light to others now has this face spat upon by the least of the least. The contrast between the absolutely good past and the absolutely bad present is total. Just as in the prologue both Job's authority and the total destruction are described in an almost exemplary way, so too they are here: the peak of respectability is replaced by the peak of injustice. At the nadir of his misery Job calls on God for help. But God does not react to Job's questions.

'I call to you fo help, but you do not answer me;
I stand there, but you do not notice me.
You have become my tyrant,
and you follow me with your powerful hand' (30.20–21).

God has changed from protector to tyrant. God is given a particular content, depending on the state of Job's life and morale. It is characteristic that the same words are always used, like guardian and guard; these take on positive ('protector') or negative ('gaoler') content depending on the context and the perspective. God assumes a face depending on the perspective from which he is looked at. It can hardly be otherwise. But the crazy thing is that people think that they can require of God a form of behaviour corresponding to their image of God. So in Job's view God must be a just king; in other words, he must be just by Job's human standards, and preferably even a bit more so.

Demands for the future

It is above all in the last part, chapter 31, that Job's line of thought really becomes clear. Job says that he has made a covenant with God and that he has in no way committed transgressions against that covenant, either in word or deed. A covenant involves taking on obligations, and that has particular consequences. If you keep to that covenant, all goes well with you; if you do not, things go badly with you. God has constantly kept an eye on Job, watched him and spied on him; he knows how irreproachable Job was and Job himself insists on his integrity from beginning to end. Now that Job has once again drawn this integrity to God's attention, he thinks that God must restore everything, and change the wretched past into a future which will be as prosperous as the past.

> 'I have made a covenant . . .
> Have I walked with falsehood,
> or has my foot hastened to lie?
> Let me be weighed in a just balance,
> and God will know my integrity . . .
> If my heart has been enticed to a woman,
> and I have lain in wait at my neighbour's door,
> then let my wife grind for another,
> and let others bow down upon her . . .
> If I have rejected the cause of my manservant or my maid-
> servant,
> when they brought a complaint against me,
> what then should I do if God were to rise up,
> when he makes inquiry, what should I answer him?' (31.1–14).

Job has tried to force God to give an account of himself by means of a lawsuit. But God has not appeared. Now Job wants to force a change through a series of oaths. Now God will have to concede Job's integrity and now he will have to meet his obligation to recompense or reward Job's behaviour justly. Job has to force God to follow the principle of recompense or moral retribution. He continues to measure by a human standard of justice.

We can see most clearly how the content which Job gives to justice goes by human criteria and how it is conditioned by its time at points where in our time and culture we adopt other views. This is immediately evident in 31.9–12. There Job says, 'If I had desired the wife of another, then I would have deserved a "just" punishment.' He then goes on to mention as a just punishment for his transgressions that his wife should go to 'grind' for other men. This amounts to saying that she must go and keep house for other men. Moreover these other men may 'bow down upon her', 'take' her or have sexual intercourse with her. According to Job, it is just for his wife to be punished for the sexual transgression of her husband. At a time when men regarded their wives as their possessions, these men developed their norms of what was just and what was not. Here we can see very clearly the difficulties attached to the demand for justice before God and the principle of moral retribution generally. The moment that one requires treatment from God which one feels to be right, one is taking one's own culture and context, one's own life and thought, and calling that a generally valid principle. We see this not only in Job's approach to his wife but also in his view of the ideal king as absolute ruler, and in his view of people who as slaves are the possessions of others. Even his picture of outcasts is conditioned by his time and place. However, this conditioning by context is true not only of Job but equally of all human beings, and thus also of our own claims and questions. For we, too, are not in a position to make demands for the whole world and all times outside ourselves; for us, too, the content of this justice is tied to time and place.

Job's integrity and persistence are necessary to make it clear to readers where the shoe pinches, namely in our idea of a fair distribution of justice. It is this image of a just distribution of money and possessions, happiness and unhappiness over the world, that we usually apply to God. Precisely by drawing extreme conclusions from it, the book of Job shows us how wrong the human idea is that we should require an account and an explanation from God, that we should want to force God to act in accordance with our own views and ideals.

The two parts of the monologue again

Together, the two parts of Job's monologue give us an insight into this phase of the process which Job is undergoing. After all the misery and dialogues, Job presents his view of human existence, of what human beings are and are not capable of doing, and of wisdom, and he spells out the insights and ideals by which he has lived. At the same time there is a marked discrepancy between the general insight of wisdom and his experience of the brokenness of his existence. Job makes that clear in the first part, the hymn of praise to wisdom. Human experiential wisdom simply indicates the need for human beings to behave in a particular way, but does not give an explanation or a justification for the creation or for the acts of God in creation. At the end of his hymn of praise Job says that one must fear God and do good. According to Job, this is all that human beings can do.

On the other hand, in his faith Job had always thought that justice was the basis for faith: if one acts well, then things go well; and if one acts badly, they go badly. What is good and bad is stated in a 'programme of faith' like the Torah or Bible. But now, we could say following Job's line, it proves that God does not keep to that programme (of faith); he regards it as a programme for human beings and not as a programme for himself. We could then ask whether human beings need to go on observing the Torah, the Bible or another programme of faith or life if it is no longer God's programme. One answer could be that it is good for people to direct their lives by such a programme, precisely because it is a good human programme, not because it is an eternally true or divine programme. In that case the Torah or the Bible (or the Qur'an) can be very meaningful as collections of human rules and give meaning to people's lives; however, this meaning does not *a priori* coincide with the meaning given by God.

But Job does not arrive at this insight. He continues to impose on God the human wisdom which is based on our principles of a just distribution and recompense. Therefore he gets nowhere. The clash between the first and second parts of the monologue reflect his impotence in this phase of his wrestling. He cannot combine the two parts as long as he remains fixed on the idea of a correspondence between the human world and God; as long as he continues to keep to the human principle of causality, retribution and justice as a universal and timeless principle for God. Job has talked himself out, for within the circle of moral retribution in which he stands, he can only keep repeating himself. He adds his signature (31.35) and utters his last words. This is also said literally at the end of this monologue (31.40): 'the words of Job are ended'. The circle is closed and he cannot get out of it. Only if God speaks can something like a solution dawn. But before that happens, another speaker appears on the scene, Elihu.

Elihu's Speech: Job 32–37

1. Then these three men ceased to answer Job, because he was righteous in his own eyes. 2. But Elihu the son of Barachel the Buzite, of the family of Ram, became angry. He was angry at Job because Job thought that he was in the right before God. 3. He was angry also at Job's three friends because they had found no answer, although they had declared Job to be in the wrong. 4. Only Elihu had waited to speak to Job because they were older than he. 5. However, when Elihu saw that the three men no longer had an answer in their mouths, he flew into a rage. 6. And Elihu the son of Barachel the Buzite answered:

'I am still young in years, and you are aged;
therefore I was timid and afraid
to declare my opinion to you.

7. I thought, "Let old age speak,
and many years teach wisdom."

8. But in reality it is the spirit in a man,
the breath of the Almighty that gives insight.

9. Length of life does not make a man wise,
and grey hairs are no guarantee of right judgment.

10. Therefore I say, "Listen to me;
let me also declare my opinion."

11. Behold, I waited for your words,
I listened for your insights,
while you sought out arguments.

12. I gave you my attention,
and, behold, no one confuted Job,
none of you answered his words.

13. Do not say, "Job was too wise for us,
only God may vanquish him, not man."

14. For I have not yet discussed with him,
and I have quite different arguments from yours.

15. There they stand now, smitten with dumbness,
no retort seems to be in them.

16. And I am just waiting; but they have no more to say,

       they stand there with their tongues in their mouths.
17. Well, now I shall say what I have to say,
      and indicate what I think.
18. I am overflowing with arguments,
      bursting with arguments;
19. my heart is seething like wine that has no vent:
      like new wineskins, it is ready to burst.
20. I must speak; that will relieve me;
      I will open my mouth and say things.
21. I will not show partiality to anyone,
      or use flattery towards any man.
22. For I do not know how to flatter,
      else my Maker would soon put an end to me.'

Job has had his say, the three friends have had their say, and we are all waiting for God. However, a totally new figure appears, Elihu. Evidently he had always been present, but kept silent. Therefore we have not been aware of him. Now he appears once, but for a long time. He introduces himself: 'I have heard all that you have said, but I have kept my mouth shut because I am much younger than you are. But now that you have finished speaking I feel that I need to say something.' That something proves to be far more than one might expect. Moreover his tone and style differs from that of his predecessors: it is more baroque, repetitive and exaggerated. All this makes Elihu's text ambiguous and explains why divergent and even contradictory readings are possible.

An ironic reading

That is certainly my portrait, says Elihu. He calls himself shy and afraid, but have you ever heard anyone operating so arrogantly? Intelligent and bombastic statements continually alternate. Elihu behaves like the familiar angry young man who knows how the world works better than his elders. No one takes so long to introduce himself. He says that he has listened carefully to the others and that he has something completely new to add. He then goes on to relate things that the three friends have also spoken about earlier. He thinks that he can see everything so clearly that he can speak in the name of God. His long and flowery introduction sets the tone for his contribution.

It looks as if the narrator wants to present him as an arrogant young fool.

But not everything that Elihu says is nonsensical. In what he says he anticipates topics which will also appear in God's speech. Is Elihu then a crazy man who now and then says profound things? Or is he perhaps not as stupid as he seems, and is it the narrator who does him down from the moment that he is introduced? In that case only the introduction by the narrator would be meant ironically, and what Elihu actually says would not be bad. However, the bombastic language which Elihu uses also prejudices the reader against him. Yet the young Elihu says a number of things that YHWH says; it is the fact that he is the onc who says them, the language that he uses and the moment at which he is introduced that make everything he says sound different. Precisely because in the divine speech YHWH is the speaker, we listen in a different way, and from the start understand what is being said in a positive light. Imagine that what is put in the mouth of God later, between chapters 38 and 41 inclusive, were put, for example, in the mouth of Job's wife. We might well then think that this text was not so good. We might also rate Elihu's text more highly were it spoken by someone else. Much of our evaluation of what someone says is based on the authority that we attribute to the speaker. Much of our assessment as readers is based on the authority attributed to a character. And so as readers we attribute more worth to Job than to his friends, and more worth to YHWH than to Elihu. Thus in the context of the book Elihu emerges as a comic figure who is made somewhat ridiculous by the author, regardless of what he actually says.

A *legal reading*

Elihu appears in his own court and alternately takes the roles of judge, public prosecutor and advocate. So he is a one-man show. However, he does not do this out of a craving for attention or a feeling that from his youth his legal talent has not been recognized. No, he is meeting Job's request for an honest trial. Job has so often asked for a lawsuit against God in which he can defend his interests. But no one has acceded to his request, neither his friends nor God. Elihu is the first to have listened to Job and satisfied this request. At the beginning of his argument Elihu explains why he is the most suitable candidate to act as an impartial judge. He is young and unprejudiced, wise and clever, and is not on the side of either Job or the friends, but on God's side. With such a qualified person the trial can hardly go wrong.

Elihu begins his work as judge in chapter 33. He summons Job to appear before him and answer his questions:

> 'Answer me, if you can!
> Present your case before me! Take the stand!
> Behold, before God I am as you are;
> I too am formed of clay.
> Look, no fear of me need terrify you;
> and my hand will not weigh heavily on you' (33.5–7).

Next Elihu takes up the accusations that Job has previously made against God. Job has said, 'God is a spy, an enemy who does not give me my rights. God is not accessible in a lawsuit, he never answers accusations and evades any judgment.' Elihu answers with a brilliant legal manoeuvre. God certainly speaks, he says, but not in a lawsuit at the gate of the city. God speaks in dreams and in physical pains. We thus have an accusation and a rebuttal, which must be adjudicated in this lawsuit.

After a quick change of clothing, Elihu appears as prosecutor. Because Job cannot expect God to appear in a lawsuit, Elihu takes on God's task: he speaks in the name of the public prosecutor (God) and accuses Job. Job as accuser is himself accused before God. Here Elihu addresses the assembled 'court' of wise men, or the jury:

> 'Hear my arguments, you men,
> and give ear to me, you who know.
> For the ear tests arguments
> as the palate tastes food.
> Let us choose for ourselves what is right;
> let us determine among ourselves what is good.
> For Job has said, "I am innocent,
> and God has taken away my right"' (34.2–5).

After appearing as Job's accuser, Elihu now turns into God's defender. Like all advocates, Elihu can speak well and so he also goes on for a long time. This defence of God occupies two chapters (36 and 37). He sums up God's great deeds and calls on Job to wonder at and praise this great God and his works.

> 'Hear this, Job;
> stop and consider the wondrous works of God.
> Do you know how God lays his command upon them
> and causes the lightning of his cloud to shine?
> Do you know the floatings of the clouds,
> the wondrous works of him who is perfect in knowledge?
> You whose garments become hot
> when the earth is still because of the south wind,
> Can you, with him, hammer the clouds flat,
> hard as a molten mirror?' (37.14–18).

Thus Elihu's argument can be read as a legal speech. Previously Job had repeatedly summoned God to appear before the court. This request for a lawsuit was even put in a document and made official with a signature (31.35). Immediately after that Elihu appears as the arbiter in the case. He summons Job before a session and rejects his accusation on the grounds that a transcendent God does not give a direct answer to human beings. After that he appears as Job's prosecutor, because Job has dared to charge God with injustice. Then he puts his demand to the local community and defends God's just governance. Finally, as judge he concludes the session with a call to Job to respect God. Elihu's argument is logical from a legal point of view and meaningful within the context of this book.

Job does not react to Elihu's mini-trial, since immediately afterwards a storm bursts. It is more than a storm, it is a force twelve whirlwind. This storm is a speech by the Almighty himself. Elihu's defence in the name of the Almighty pales beside it. This demotes Elihu in the eyes of the readers of the book of Job, so that they are inclined to regard him as worthless and of no value. Thus the author not only gives an ironic twist to his argument by putting Elihu's appearance the moment after the conclusion of the dialogues and Job's monologue. He makes even more of a mock of Elihu's legal pretentions by the appearance of God which immediately follows.

A prophetic reading

Elihu is convinced that he is speaking in the name of God. He does not want to be wise as a human being, since he is still young and inexperienced. But he does want to be wise as a prophet, as someone who is inspired by God. Seven times he mentions that he has to explain why Job and the audience must listen to him. In this respect his name, too, is significant, since Elihu is very like the name of the prophet Eliyahu or Elijah, the prophet who spoke in the name of God and who will return as forerunner of the day of YHWH. Elihu too speaks in God's name, and God's appearance in the storm wind directly after Elihu's speech makes Elihu God's forerunner.

Elihu has an optimistic view of life. That is understandable for a young man, and he also has this view as a prophet. All suffering has a purpose, he says. God speaks in that suffering and thus warns people against arrogance. Unlike Job's friends, Elihu does not explain suffering in terms of its cause, but in terms of its purpose. He does not accept the principle that a bad life leads to suffering. Suffering has the specific function of making people think, of turning moments of crisis into moments of salvation and teaching people to review their lives. This appeal makes Elihu's message tolerable and optimistic, all the more so since he associates with this appeal a call to worship God and wonder at all the marvellous works of his creation.

> 'The Almighty, we cannot find him;
> great in power and justice,
> with abundant righteousness
> he does not answer.
> Therefore men fear him;
> he does not regard any who are
> wise in their own conceit' (37.23–24).

Despite repeated requests from Elihu, Job does not react. Who can refute a prophet? After all, he is speaking in the name of God and it is difficult to contradict him. Prophets are accepted or opposed. They are listened to or silenced. Job has listened and keeps quiet. In his monologue he had already come to the conclusion that to fear God is the only thing a person can do (chapter 28), and here he agrees with the prophetic element in Elihu. Precisely in this respect the two anticipate what God is going to say in the storm. When God himself speaks immediately afterwards, he not only challenges his opponents to review their allegations but also makes even his most fervent defenders look foolish. That is the fate of Elihu, the judge and prophet.

The place of Elihu's speech in the book of Job

Elihu's speech raises difficulties in any division of the book of Job. Does this speech belong with the dialogues or with God's speech? I think that the ironical, legal and prophetic readings together can give an answer to the question of the place and function of Elihu's speech in the book. The ironic reading shows the separate position of Elihu's argument: following the dialogues and monologue unexpectedly and immediately followed by God's speech, this witness stands apart and functions without any direct relationship to the surrounding context. The legal reading shows the agreements between Elihu's speech and what Job's friends say. He resembles them in his pessimistic assessment of Job. Like them he also defends God's just governance and calls on Job to praise God instead of accusing him of injustice. By contrast, the prophetic reading points forward to God's speech. In his optimistic look at life, even at Job's life, he sketches a picture of the totality of creation which resembles the pictures which will appear in God's speech. Could it not be that, like Job's monologue, Elihu's speech performs the function of a hinge? That would explain the remarkable place of Elihu's speech after both the speeches of the friends and Job's monologue, and immediately before God's speech. The place of the speech between dialogue and 'theologue' is then a sign of the bridging function that Elihu's argument fulfils. Along with Job's second monologue this speech by Elihu would then form a hinge. It is also striking that there are parallels between Job's monologue and Elihu's speech. In his hymn of praise to wisdom Job recognizes that human beings can do a great deal, but do not have a monopoly of wisdom. Only God knows the place of wisdom. Job ends his hymn of praise with a call to fear God.

Elihu celebrates God's omnipotence in a similar way to Job, albeit in a more prophetic framework. He ends by saying: 'Therefore men fear the Almighty, and even those who are wise in their hearts cannot see him.' In their description of the creation both anticipate God's speech, but in addition Job in his second monologue refers back to the things which he himself had said earlier in his dialogues with his friends, whereas Elihu primarily refers back to elements of the dialogue which the three friends had spoken. Thus it can become clear that only after Elihu's speech is there a complete hinge between the central panel of the triptych with the dialogues and the third panel with God's speech.

God's Speech, Part One: Job 38–40.5

There is no wind, and the air is vibrating in the heat of the day. No birds are singing, not a sound is to be heard. But there is an inexpressible tension in the air. The people have talked themselves out: Job, his friends and also the strange guest Elihu. They don't expect anything more. They are sitting down, each wrapped up in himself. Suddenly the wind gets up. At first they are pleased and think, 'Good, a gentle breeze.' But rapidly the breeze proves to be a hurricane which sucks up everything in its wake. In a few seconds all the dwellings and coverings that human beings have constructed on the earth have been torn from their places. This storm is God's reaction, his answer to Job. Like a whirlwind he plucks up all the plans and ideas of Job and his friends, lifts them into the air and smashes them down again to earth. And after that everything is different from before.

1. YHWH answered Job out of the whirlwind and said,
2. 'Who is this that darkens my governance
   by arguments without knowledge?
3. Gird up your loins like a man,
   I will question you, and you shall answer me.
4. Where were you when I laid the foundation of the earth?
   Tell me, if you have understanding.
5. Who determined its measurements? Surely you know!
   Who stretched the line upon it?
6. On what were its pillars sunk?
   Who laid its cornerstone,
7. when the morning stars sang together
   and all the sons of God shouted for joy?
8. Who hedged round the sea with doors,
   when it appeared from the womb;
9. when I clothed it in clouds,
   and swaddled it in thick darkness,

10. when I prescribed bounds for it,
    set bars and doors

11. and said, "Thus far and no further,
    here shall your proud waves be halted"?

12. Have you ever commanded the morning in all your days,
    and shown the dawn its place,

13. that it might take hold of the skirts of the earth
    and shake the wicked out of it?

14. It (the earth) changes like clay under the seal,
    even its colours, like those of a garrnent.

15. The evildoers are robbed of their light,
    their uplifted arm is broken.

16. Have you penetrated to the springs of the sea,
    or have you walked in the recesses of the deep?

17. Are the gates of death accessible to you,
    or have you ever seen the gates of darkness?

18. Have you discerned the extent of the earth?
    Say so, if you know all this.

19. Where is the way to the dwelling of light,
    and darkness, where is its place?

20. Then you can bring it home,
    and show it the way.

21. You will know that, since you were born so long ago,
    and the number of your days is so great.

22. Have you penetrated to the storehouses of the snow,
    have you seen the treasuries of the hail,

23. which I reserve for difficult times,
    for days of battle and war?

24. Where is the way to the place where the light is divided,
    from where the east wind is scattered upon the earth?

25. Who has cleft a channel for the torrents of rain?
    Who has levelled a path for the rolling thunder,

26. to pour rain down on an uninhabited land,
    on a desert where no human being is,

27. to drench the waste and desolate land,
    and to make grass sprout even there?

28. Has the rain a father?
    Who has begotten the dewdrops?

29. From whose womb did the ice come forth?
    Who has given birth to the hoarfrost of heaven,

30. when the waters strangely become icy stone,
    and the face of the deep is frozen?

31. Can you bind the chains of the Pleiades,
    or loose the cords of Orion?
32. Can you lead forth Mazzarot in its time,
    or lead the Bear with its children?
33. Do you know the laws of the heavens?
    Determine their rule on the earth?
34. When you cry a command to the clouds,
    does the kindly rain stream over you?
35. When you command the lightning to come,
    does it say, 'Here we are'?
36. Who has put wisdom in the clouds?
    Who gave insight to the mist?
37. Who can number the clouds by wisdom,
    or who can tilt the waterskins of the heavens,
38. so that the dust flows together like a moulding
    and the clods stick to each other?
39. Can you hunt prey for the lioness,
    and satisfy the appetite of her hungry whelps,
40. when they crouch in their hiding places,
    to lie in wait under the bushes?
41. Who provides for the raven its prey,
    when its young ones cry to God,
    and wander about for lack of food?'

The structure and tone of God's speech

Like a cyclone or whirlwind, God's stormy speech has a clear structure. After the opening sentence God asks Job a great many questions, and these are about the whole of creation. The first questions are about the earth, its foundations, the sea and the continents. This cosmogony is followed by questions about the weather, the wind and heavenly bodies. Finally follow questions about all kinds of different animals, which form a sort of bestiary. All of this together makes up the first part of God's speech. The second part of God's argument (40–41) focusses on two animals which by their size and impressiveness put all other animals in the shade: Behemoth and Leviathan. Perhaps readers think that God is not really giving any answer at all to the questions and problems which Job and his friends have raised. They may secretly think that he is blustering a bit, imposing himself and asking cynical questions. Or, 'If I were God sitting in a comfortable chair and looking down from above at the goings-on of human beings on earth, I too would talk like that.' But the question is whether God really is failing to give an answer to the questions which have been put to him.

The fact that God is 'revealing' himself and answering counts, but very soon the 'tone of the music' counts even more. In this case it is the poetic forms and imagery which colour and ultimately even define the revelation. It is above all the poetic beauty and the wealth of idiom which make God's speech the climax to the book of Job. It is as if we are standing before the panorama of creation and then can even look at it through God's eyes. In addition there is the imposing and sometimes even mocking tone of an almighty God who keeps saying, 'Give me an answer, you know it so well!' That gives these poetic images a touch of irony. Moreover God's whole speech from the storm proves not only to have its own effective structure but also to form the well-considered climax to a development of images, ideas and themes which occurred earlier in the book. Everything comes together here and finds its climax. The poetry of God's speech is so strongly bound up with what has gone before that it is a fulfilment of the key passages in the book. And then, if we have an eye for the matching imagery, we see that in substance God is also reacting to the dialogues between Job and his friends and the monologues of Job himself.

God's speech as a reaction to the dialogues

In addition to new and striking ideas, God also takes up imagery with which Job and his friends are already familiar. The tone and colour which God gives to them and the total perspective in which he puts them gives these old insights a new weight in his speech. By looking at some of the images we can see the agreements and differences between elements in the argument of Eliphaz, Zophar and Job and those in God's speech.

'Think now! What innocent person has ever perished?
Where were the upright cut off?
As I have seen, those who plough iniquity and sow trouble

reap the same.
By the breath of God they perish,
and by the blast of his anger they are consumed.
The lion can roar and growl,
the teeth of the young lion are broken.
The lion perishes for lack of prey,
and the whelps of the lioness are scattered' (4.10–11).

The same animal, the lion, appears in God's speech:

'Can you hunt prey for the lioness,
and satisfy the appetite her hungry whelps,
when they crouch in their hiding places,
to lie in wait under the bushes?' (38.39–40).

These images, taken from the same world, describe the lioness
and her young. But they are used to support very different assertions. Eliphaz uses them to emphasize that there is a firm connection between action and consequences and expresses that
as 'What you sow, you shall reap.' He uses the picture of the
roaring lion to indicate the contrast: with God's help it is
possible to cope with such a powerful animal and such a wicked
man, however powerful. For Eliphaz the comparison supports
his defence of moral retribution: live well, so that you reap, and
if the breath of God falls on you, all will come out right. Here he
uses the image of the lion(ess) to make God's punishment more
impressive. In God's speech the image of the lioness shows how,
as one of the animals created by God, she can look after herself
and her young. God brings the lioness on the scene to depict his
own work of creation and the self-sufficiency of his creation.
The picture which in Eliphaz's speech serves to support the
meaning of moral retribution functions in God's speech as one
example in the whole of God's creation.

In the first dialogue between Bildad and Job, Bildad above all
uses botanical images. These do not appear in God's speech. By
contrast Zophar uses cosmic images which do show a similarity
to God's speech:

'Can you find out the deep things of God?
Can you find out the limit of the Almighty?
It is higher than heaven – what can you do?

Deeper than She'ol – what can you know of it?
Its measure is longer than the earth,
broader than the sea.
If he (God) storms in, imprisons
and calls to judgment, who can resist him?
For he knows unjust men
and he sees iniquity; can he not discern it?' (11.7–11).

In his speech God is also concerned with the role of the deep,
the abyss or primal sea.

'Where were you when I laid the foundation of the earth?
Tell me, if you have understanding.
Who determined its measurements? Surely you know!
Who stretched the line upon it?
Have you penetrated to the springs of the sea,
or have you walked in the recesses of the deep?' (38.4–5,16).

Zophar speaks of God's unfathomable nature and omnipotence. The stereotyped character of Zophar's language and its clichés are immediately clear: 'higher than the heaven, deeper than the underworld' is a description of God which often occurs. Zophar speaks truths which come (too) easily from his mouth. It is more crucial that Zophar quickly makes a move, which is obvious to him, from this almighty God to God as a judge who condemns and punishes. For him moral retribution and God's omnipotence are indissolubly connected. If you believe in God as creator, then you believe in God as a judge who punishes. In God's speech this cliché is burst open and the superficiality and ease of speaking are not there. God does not compare himself with the sea or with any height or depth. In contrast to human beings, he has insight into them, since he established them, but he preserves a certain distance from what he has made. God and Zophar make use of the same image of the depths and the sea, but Zophar uses them to indicate God's creation and control, while God uses this picture only to refer to his act of creation and human ignorance, without any connection with control or retribution.

Not only the friends, but Job make use of images which similarly echo in God's speech. As with Eliphaz and Zophar, they take on a different meaning through their new context.

> 'He removes mountains from their place and they know it
> not,
> in his anger he overturns them.
> He shakes the earth out of its place
> and its pillars tremble.
> He commands the sun and it does not rise;
> he covers up the stars.
> He alone spreads out the heavens
> and walks over the waves of the sea.
> He made the Great Bear and Orion,
> the Pleiades and the stars of the south.
> Great, unfathomable things he brings into being,
> innumerable wondrous works.
> Behold, he passes me by and I do not see him;
> he slips past me, and I do not notice him.
> Behold, when he strikes, who will prevent him?'

Compare this with God's speech in 38.31–33:

> 'Can you bind the chains of the Pleiades,
> or loose the cords of Orion?
> Can you lead forth Mazzarot in its time,
> or lead the Bear with its children?
> Do you know the laws of the heavens?
> Determine their rule on the earth?'

In the dialogues Job has not just said good things, nor have the friends just said bad things. By thinking and feeling on the basis of his experience, Job comes to produce less trite formulations and images than his friends. He formulates insights which closely resemble those expressed by God. At the same time, what Job says comes within a process of growth and setbacks, so that these insights are often embedded in a context of doubt or desperation. This is very clear in 9.5–10, where Job's recognition of God's creative power goes with assertions about God's fury and anger. For Job, God's greatness is at the same time both wonderful and terrifying, and above all unfathomable. Job complains about this incalculable God, whom he neither understands nor sees. In his answer God mentions almost the same images as Job, like the Great Bear, Orion and the Pleiades, although he also mentions the constellation Mazzarot, which is unknown to us. In this way God shows Job that he can be discovered in the wonderful works of creation which Job sees around him every day. They present the order which God has thoughtfully established in creation. God cites the same creation which for Job indicates both God's wisdom and God's arbitrariness as a proof of his wisdom and his order.

Both the agreements in imagery and the differing use and divergent evaluation of these images show precisely the problem that the book of Job is about. Human beings see the creation that God sees. But whereas in the theatre of creation human beings have a seat at the back of the gallery, God sits in the stalls. Human beings see the stage from a limited perspective; they cannot see parts of the stage and often they can only see the actors' feet. By contrast, as director and producer God sits in the first row and can see the whole stage from one wing to the other. This difference in position leads to insoluble problems for human beings, since they are not in a position to understand everything. The dialogue between Job and his friends at the back of the gallery shows what solutions human beings think compensate for their limited view. Like Job's friends, they often play God. They then act as if they could survey the whole world and 'explain' incomprehensible suffering from a divine perspective which they have adopted.

God's speech as a reaction to Job's first monologue

The agreements in imagery and terminology in Job's first monologue and God's answer in chapter 38 are so numerous that God's speech seem to be a direct answer to the questions raised there. This is not so strange when we reflect that in his first monologue Job, under the utmost provocation, has raised his key questions. God's speech from the storm is a direct reaction to these questions.

In Job's heartfelt cry, all the attention was focussed on the pain within him. His monologue took us to the innermost core of his grief. He wanted to detach himself from the outside world as far as possible. He has already seen and experienced too much and therefore wants no longer to exist. He would much prefer to be imprisoned in darkness, to return to the womb and keep all the doors shut. And as far as he is concerned, these doors may remain shut for ever. Over against this we have God's poem, the picture of a panoramic view. Instead of expressing a desire for death, every verse expresses vitality, insight into the activity of life. Beginning with gripping images about the creation of the world, God shows how the world is kept in being by natural forces and finally the whole variety of the animal kingdom. Whereas Job's camera was focussed on deep darkness and the innermost depths, God's camera pans from high to low, over the whole breadth of creation: air and sea, snow and wind, heavenly bodies; from inhabited land and the plains on which only wild animals dwell to the land inhabited by human beings. This general shift from Job's fixation on death to a fixation on life through God is carefully developed in detail, image by image, in God's argument.

Job's monologue begins with a series of urgent wishes. He wants the day to disappear and be replaced by the night; light must be swallowed up by the darkness.

'Woe is the day on which I was born,
and the night which said "a boy has been conceived".
That day should have remained darkness' (3.2–4a).

God begins his speech with the same theme of 'darkening':

'Who is this that darkens my governance
by arguments without knowledge?

Where were you when I laid the foundation of the earth?
Tell me, if you have understanding . . .
Who laid its cornerstone,
when the morning stars sang together
and all the sons of God shouted for joy?
Who hedged round the sea with doors,
when it appeared from the womb;
when I clothed it in clouds,
and swaddled it in thick darkness,
when I prescribed bounds for it,
set bars and doors

and said, "Thus far and no further,
here shall your proud waves be halted"?
Have you penetrated to the springs of the sea.
or have you walked in the recesses of the deep?
Are the gates of death accessible to you,
or have you ever seen the gates of darkness?' (Job 38.4–17).

For God, the theme of darkening forms the summary or the
nucleus of his accusation against Job: he accuses Job of 'darkening' his governance. Over against Job's need for darkness, God
emphasizes both day and night. Job begs for night, darkness and
shadows of death: 'darken the morning stars so that they give
no more light.' God makes the same morning stars indicate the
beginning of the day of creation. Sound is judged in a similar
way. Job acknowledges that as a new-born child he cried out at
birth, but now he wants to undo this birth-cry retrospectively,
and exchange it for the lamentations over the dead. God sets
over against this the jubilant cries of the morning stars and the
joyful decrees of the sons of God, who celebrate the beginning
of creation and birth. Another picture which both Job and God
use but evaluate totally differently is that of the 'clouds'. Job
asks for clouds to cover and darken the day on which he was
born: 'May darkness and the shadow of death claim the day of
my birth, may clouds veil it.' In God's speech the clouds form
the swaddling clothes of creation. Whereas for Job the clouds
function as a kind of shroud and are thus in the context of
death, God makes them serve as swaddling clothes for the newly
born and stand in the framework of birth. Thus God confronts
Job with the same images, but reverses them. Job wants to shift
the balance between two basic principles of creation, light and
darkness, in the direction of darkness. God maintains the
balance between light and darkness.

One striking image is that of doors or gates. Job says that he
would have preferred the doors or gates of his mother's womb
to have remained shut at his birth. Now that he has been born
he asks to see the gates of death or the underworld as quickly as
possible. This twofold function of the gate as an entry into life
and an exit to death recurs in God's speech in a special way.
God says that he is the one who at creation first opened the

gates for the primal sea, who hammered on the gates of the womb to open it. But God also says that later he has closed these gates again and limited the sea with floodgates, so that other life becomes possible. For God 'gate' then means protection and barrier at the same time; opening and closing make life possible. On the other hand God also knows the gates of the underworld, which serve to protect death against life. Thus by means of gates God also ensures a protection from death and a barrier for it. In short, life and death are both made possible and maintained by God.

God's radically different view of creation

For his answer to Job God chooses the arena of creation and not the palace of justice, although in the dialogue Job had often asked for the latter. Job's challenge to God was very radical, but now it proves that God's answer is no less radical. Everywhere else in the Hebrew Bible human beings are the crown of creation, meant to rule over nature. That perhaps explains why there is little nature poetry in the Hebrew Bible: the world of nature is intrinsically of little significance; it arises only when human beings appear in it. However, from this speech by God it proves that the world of nature is itself valuable. Here human beings stand on the periphery of this world, thundered over by natural forces which cannot be subjugated and animals which cannot be tamed. This is diametrically opposed to the creation story in Genesis 1, which talks about the creation in six days and in which the creation of human beings forms the climax (Gen.1.27–28):

> 'So God created man in his own image,
> in the image of God he created him,
> male and female he created them.
> And God blessed them and said to them:
> "Be fruitful and multiply,
> fill the earth and subdue it
> rule over the fishes of the sea
> and over the birds of the heaven
> and over all the animals that move over the earth." '

In the story of the Garden of Eden (Genesis 2–3), too, all the attention is focussed on human beings: on human beings who must till the earth, on the man and the woman, and on human beings in relation to the animals. However broadly creation is established, everything is related to human beings.

Moreover the readers of God's speech in the book of Job in the first instance expect the same picture of creation, in which much attention is paid to human beings, who are given the ethical task of living well and serving God. How amazed they must be when it proves that in his account of creation in Job God does not mention human beings at all. He describes the earth, the sea, the heavenly bodies, the weather and the wind and . . . numerous animals; but he does not mention human beings. Here they do not at all seem to stand at the centre of creation but at the periphery. And that when human beings think that they are the measure of all things.

You might almost come to the conclusion that God is far more interested in animals than in human beings. God doesn't mention human beings, but functions as a guide in a safari park. He sums up animals with their own characteristics:

> 'Who provides for the raven its prey,
> when its young ones cry to God,
> and wander about for lack of food?' (38.41).

> 'Do you know when the mountain goats bring forth?
> Do you watch over the calving of the hinds?
> Do you count the months that they must fulfil?
> Do you know the time when they bring forth?
> They crouch, bring forth their offspring,
> and are delivered of their young.
> Their young ones become strong and grow up in the open;
> they run away, and do not return to them' (39.1–4).

> 'Is it by your wisdom that the hawk soars,
> and spreads his wings towards the south?
> Is it at your command that the eagle mounts up
> and makes his nest on high?
> He nestles and sleeps on a rock,
> the peak of a rock is his fortress.

Thence he spies out the prey;
his eyes behold it afar off.
His young ones suck up blood;
and where the slain are, there is he' (39.26–30).

Have you ever read such an unsentimental poem about the animal world? And it comes out of God's mouth! This speech by God does not contain any sentimental stuff about lovely birds and dear little monkeys and pussy cats, but pictures of animals for whom the task of looking after their young involves devouring other animals and sucking up blood from corpses. With great matter-of-factness, here God presents a picture of the daily rhythm of life and death, a rhythm that keeps itself in being and lacks any kind of moralizing human interpretation.

A line runs from God's depiction of the inanimate world, with land and sea, weather and wind, to this portrayal of the animal kingdom. The great terrifying forces of the natural world correspond to the violence of the animals, and both escape any human influence. And yet God keeps all this in being! He supports a continual renewal of life, which includes a continual annihilation of life:

'The wings of the ostrich wave proudly;
but are they truly lovely pinions and plumage?
For she leaves her eggs on the ground,
and lets them be warmed in the dust.
She forgets that a foot may crush them,
or that a wild beast may trample them.
She deals cruelly with her young,
as if they were not hers;
she is not troubled
that her labour may be in vain.
For God has robbed her of wisdom,
and given her no share in understanding.
But when she rouses herself,
she laughs at the horse and his rider' (39.13–18).

Nature is not a mechanical event in which everything takes place automatically and without choices or insights. The impulse to propagate and to feed oneself depends on the wisdom with which God has provided every living being. The ostrich has more instinct than insight; human beings have more insight, but no wisdom that surveys everything. However, both know how to act. All, both animals and human beings, are in a position to act in accordance with their own natures and capacities. That also emerges from the description of the following animals:

'Who has let the wild ass go free?
Who has loosed the bonds of the swift ass,
to whom I have given the steppe for his home,
and the salt land for his dwelling place?
He scorns the tumult of the city,
he does not hear the shouts of a driver.
He ranges the mountains as his pasture,
and he searches after every green thing' (39.5–8).

'Do you give the horse his might?
Do you lead his neck with thunder?
Do you make him leap like the locust?
His majestic snorting is terrible.
He paws violently,
and exults in his strength
and rushes to meet the weapons.
He laughs at fear, and knows no anxiety;
he does not turn back from the sword . . .
He smells the battle from afar,
the thunder of the captains,
and the shouting' (39.19–22, 25).

Even animals like the ass and the horse which human beings are so fond of seeing as dependent on them are described as autonomous animals. They themselves, and not human beings, determine their wishes, desires and behaviour. The horse with all his power, which in battle is normally subject to the rider, is here described as an animal which goes on to the battlefield of his own free will. He goes for his own pleasure. The horse, *the* picture of combative energy and power, does not show this energy through or for human beings, but purely and solely for himself.

There is good reason for God's speech to come out of the

storm: the tone and images are not those of a gentle cooling breeze, but those of a whirlwind which knocks everything over. This argument gives us a glimpse of a world which is not supported by straightforward moral categories. Already in its storminess and whirlwind power, God's speech shows how the immense power and violence form part of the creation itself. The world persists in a continuous alternation of renewed and nourishing life on the one hand and the violence of war and death on the other. God's answer is not an easy answer, far less a direct answer to Job's question why good people have to suffer. God presents a vision of a cosmic order which in its own way is in balance, though this balance does not seem to human beings to be an ideal one. For violence is intrinsically present in nature, and annihilation is an indissoluble part of creation. This divine view confronts Job with the limits of the traditional moral imagination, as expressed by Job and his friends.

Embedded pictures

All these pictures of animals, the cosmos or meteorological phenomena are embedded in a long series of rhetorical questions which God puts to Job. 'Who are you to think that you grasp something of "my governance" or of the creation? Do you have the right to speak? Is your knowledge and ability like that of God? Who do you think you are in comparison to God?' These questions are about the relationship between God and human beings and show the contrast there is between God and Job, between God and human beings. God knows everything, human beings know nothing. This series of questions forms the framework or setting, while the creatures who are depicted are what is framed, the picture itself. The embedded pictures of creation give content to the framework of questions, to the relationship between God and human beings. In other words, the relationship between God and human beings derives form and content from the creation that is depicted. So when God shows the whole breadth of creation in his portrayal of it, he shows the whole scale of possibilities offered by creation. It is characteristic of God's painter's hand ('this is a real "God"') that both constructive and destructive forces exist side by side. In contrast to Job, who in his first monologue opts only for death, or in contrast to many people who opt only for life, the fierce colours of God's creation shine with an intensity which consists in the grace of both life and death, creation and annihilation.

Both the lists of questions and the pictures embedded in them form the first part of God's answer to the problems posed earlier. Job and his friends held on to a simple moral balance: bad people deserve darkness; good people rightly bask in the daylight. When Job finds himself in a wretched state, he begins to ask for all the forms of darkness. He asks not to be born but to die, for the sun and the stars to be darkened. God reacts to this and says: 'Have you any idea of what the full extent of light means and what kind of moral power you must have to maintain this rhythm of day and night? Isn't far more moral courage needed for an alternation of good and evil than you can conceive with your simple arithmetic? Isn't it too simple to suppose that one grants light only to good people and only darkness to bad people? It is not even right to associate all the good in creation with me and to dissociate the evil from me? Even I comprise light and darkness, good and evil. You and your friends have wanted to impose your ideal of pure good without evil on me. However, I know that only the balance between the two poles of good and evil and life and death make possible an intensity of both life and justice.'

Job's brief reaction

'Then Job answered YHWH and said,
"Behold, I am insignificant,
what can I answer you?
I lay my hand on my mouth.
I have spoken once,
I shall not answer;
twice, I shall add nothing to it"' (40.3–5).

Job, who had always said too much, now puts his hand on his mouth in awe and dismay. Not once, but twice, he has challenged God to a lawsuit, and he has accused God of a supposed offence. Confronted with the creation and able to get just a glimpse of the great work, Job says that he has no more to say.

God's Speech, Part Two: Job 40–41

God seems to have yet more to say. Job's brief reaction does not really add anything; it is more an interlude which allows God to take breath. God continues his argument about the animals, but at the same time also goes more into the questions of justice and morality.

Two impressive animals

'Behold, Behemoth, which I have made as I have made you;
he eats grass like an ox.
Behold, his strength in his loins,
and his power in the muscles of his belly.
He makes his tail stiff like a cedar;
the sinews of his thighs are knit together.
His bones are tubes of bronze;
his limbs like bars of iron . . .
Under the lotus plants he lies down,
in a hiding place of reeds and marsh . . .
If the river becomes turbulent he is not frightened;
he remains unmoved when the Jordan surges against his mouth.
Who can catch him by his eyes,
or pierce his nose with wooden pins?' (40.15–24).

Leviathan and Behemoth are the best-known chaos or primal monsters, and God introduces them in his speech as the counterparts of creation. They are the chaos monsters who are present in creation. The word Behemoth, literally 'animal' or 'large animal', denotes both the mythological primal monster which already existed before creation and continues to lead a slumbering existence, and an animal which actually exists, the hippopotamus.

God gives a splendid description of Behemoth. Because he
has not been tamed by human beings, the hippopotamus is the
prototype of a free and powerful animal. What is striking in
this description of Behemoth is the paradoxical combination
of his peaceful nature – he eats grass, lies peacefully among
the reeds – and his terrifying power. The description of his
physical build refers above all to his bones and sinews and
emphasizes his great sexual capacity. The Hebrew text puts this
in a humorous way. What the text actually has is 'he makes his
tail stiff like a cedar'. Now anyone who knows the hippopotamus's tail knows that this cannot be the case. The little
stumpy tail of the hippopotamus does not bear the slightest
resemblance to a cedar of Lebanon. The 'tail' is a euphemistic
reference to the hippopotamus's penis.

Last in the series of animals, which increases in impressiveness, God describes Leviathan at length. He is reckoned to be
the most imposing animal.

'Can you draw out Leviathan with a fishhook?
Can you press down his tongue with a cord?
Can you put a ring through his nose,
or pierce his jaw with a hook?' (40.25–26).

'Who can strip off his outer garment?
Who can penetrate his double coat of mail?
Who can open the doors of his face?
Round about his teeth is terror.
His back is made of rows of shields,
shut up with a thick seal.
One is so near to another
that no air can come between them . . .
His nostrils flash forth light,
and his eyes are like the pupils of the dawn.
His breath kindles coals,
and a flame comes forth from his mouth . . .
No one on earth can overcome him;
he is made without fear.
He beholds everything that is high;
he is king over all the sons of pride' (41.5–13, 25–26).

Leviathan, too, denotes both a mythological primal monster and an animal which really exists, namely the crocodile. A vivid description of the crocodile is given here, with all its wonderful and terrifying properties like scales, teeth and the capacity to swim. From mouth and teeth, from skin and eyes to the fire-breathing mouth, from top to toe he says one thing: 'I am unconquerable.' Moreover in the last line God calls the crocodile 'the king of beasts'. In his very first monologue Job called Leviathan a chaos monster, the counterpart of creation. From God's speech it emerges that this chaos monster continues to exist in and alongside creation. Thus creation does not exclude chaos, but includes it.

Leviathan brings the impressive list of animals to an end. Job asked God why he had to lose his wealth, children and health. God's answers put Job in a position to see further than his human nose and gives him a glimpse of the immense world of power, beauty and violence. This world is permeated by God's order. Nevertheless chaos continues to exist in this creation. For human eyes this makes the world a mass of contradictions. It offers human beings a wide scale of possibilities which comprises all the extremes from beauty to ugliness, from life to death, from hope to despair, from order to chaos, from creation to destruction, without human beings being able to get a grip on it. Job certainly did not get the answer he expected, but an answer of a very different kind.

God's speech as a reaction to Job's second monologue

In his second monologue Job sang a song of praise to wisdom and at the same time summoned God to appear before the judgment seat to give him compensation. This monologue is as it were Job's last will and testament; he himself puts his signature to it. God reacts to both parts of this monologue in his speech. God speaks about knowledge in a way which strongly resembles Job's monologue on wisdom. In his hymn Job recognizes that wisdom is the ordering principle of God's creative process, the hidden design behind everything. He recognizes that God is the only one to have seen wisdom and to have put her throughout creation. Job says that wisdom is the fundamental governing principle of the world, but that it is invisible to the human eye and incomprehensible to the human mind. All the wisdom and knowledge that human beings can acquire is 'second-hand' knowledge. God says something similar in his speech. Here he gives wisdom another name and does not speak of 'knowledge' or 'wisdom' but of *etsa*, his system or master plan. In a series of rhetorical questions God asks whether Job has knowledge of this divine plan for creation. Indirectly, here he is talking about what Job had already recognized in his hymn of praise to wisdom: human beings have no insight into others than themselves; they have no insight into the cosmos and the weather, the animals and their propagation. All creatures can utilize the possibilities in creation, but they must not think, like Job and his friends, that they know the blueprint or building plan of the world, far less that they can determine the planning of it all. Thus both God and Job recognize that only God has true knowledge or insight into the plan, *etsa*, of creation, In chapter 28 Job draws the conclusion from this that human beings must fear God. God does not refer to this in his speech from the storm.

Thus Job's monologue and God's speech do not differ in their view of knowledge of the universe, but they do differ over the connection between this wisdom (from a human perspective) or *etsa* (from God's perspective) and the idea of justice. It is this connection which God disputes. God opposes the view which Job expressed most evocatively in the second part of his second monologue. Here Job declares that he has made a covenant with God and that he has not transgressed against this covenant in anything, whether in his words and actions, or in his thoughts and wishes. Therefore he thinks that God, too, should keep this covenant. By means of a series of oaths Job wants to compel God to act 'justly'. This series of oaths clearly shows the extent to which Job's image of justice goes by human standards and is conditioned by his time. For example, according to Job, it is just for his wife to be punished for the sexual transgressions of her husband; it is just for the king to have absolute power over his subjects and for a slave to be utterly the possession of someone else. God gives an answer to this in his speech and makes it clear why the principle of moral retribution is fundamentally unsuitable as a criterion for God. By asking God for justice as they understand it, human beings are putting themselves at the centre of creation and elevating their own lives to be a norm and their thoughts to be universally valid principles. In so doing they completely fail to do justice not only to the freedom of animals and the whole of creation, but also to God's freedom. They make their own free and limited view a necessity for all others. Job criticizes God's capriciousness. God now says that it is equally capricious when human beings want to impose their perspective and vision on everyone else, and even on God. Moral retribution wrongly presupposes that human beings can establish their own view, which is contingent and contextual, as transcendent and absolute.

This is described most sharply in the most biting part of God's speech:

> 'YHWH answered Job out of the storm wind and said:
> "Gird up your loins like a man:
> I am going to question you,
> and you will give me information.
> Will you even put me in the wrong?
> Will you condemn me
> that you may be justified?
> Have you an arm like that of God?
> Can you thunder with a voice like his?
> Deck yourself with majesty and dignity;
> clothe yourself with glory and splendour.
> Pour forth the overflowings of your anger.
> Look on every one that is proud and abase him.
> Look on every one that is proud and bring him low;
> Tread down the wicked where they stand.
> Hide them all in the dust together,
> bind their faces in the hidden place.
> Then will I also honour you,
> because your own right hand gives you victory"' (40.6–14)

God does not put any more questions to Job about the world, but about himself: 'Job, you aren't in a position to answer my questions about the world. Are you going to keep on challenging me and summoning me to a law suit? Are you going to keep on imposing your human perspective on me? Are you then privy to the divine plan and knowledge of how to govern the world? If so, here is my sceptre. Take it and I shall acknowledge your power.' Job and God of course know that Job does not have this divine knowledge and power, that Job cannot share the divine perspective or adopt it.

God's radically different view of justice

God's voice from the storm blows everything over. His speech presents a radically different view of creation and a radically different view of justice from that of Job and his friends. A passage from God's speech will dot the i's here:

> 'Who has cleft a channel for the torrents of rain?
> Who has levelled a path for the rolling thunder,
> to pour rain down on an uninhabited land,
> on a desert where no human being is,
> to drench the waste and desolate land,
> and to make grass sprout even there?
> Has the rain a father?
> Who has begotten the dewdrops?' (38.25–28).

God describes the rain and says, 'Just look, Job, precious rain which people wait for to fall is spilt on land where no one lives and where no one can live.' Rain, which in the Bible is normally a clear vehicle of reward and punishment, i.e. is given for good deeds and withheld for bad deeds, is by no means a vehicle of morality. God is not speaking about rain which falls both on uninhabited land and on land where people are living. No, three times we are told that it rains on uninhabited land, desert, waste and desolate land, and not once is there a reference to rain which falls on inhabited land. How can God make it clearer that for him ethical categories of reward and punishment have nothing to do with the creation? This is God's polemic with Job: from God's perspective, human beings are marginal not only in creation, but also to moral categories.

God repeatedly says that Job does not know the foundations and corner-stones on which the world rests, the blueprint or plan. Why then should he think that the moral ideas or the idea of justice that he has always had is the basis of God's system?

God has ordered the world, and this order also seems to comprise chaos. Thus violence seems to be present in nature and destruction to be an indissoluble part of creation. Good and bad, justice and injustice, are both fundamental facts in the world: the sun rises on both sinners and pious, good people and bad people. There is no retribution of the kind that human beings would like. Justice has not been woven as a pattern into the garment of the world, nor is God burdened with its administration. It is an ideal that must be realized by human beings within their society, through them and for them, and it cannot be put to God's account.

But why is all this to be seen as gloomy and not as 'good news'? We are so used to a world in which human beings have a central place that we feel it to be a lack of justice when we can no longer refer to God. We can no longer feel wronged and says, 'God, things are not shared out fairly in the world, do something about it.' No, if we want things to be different we must act ourselves. In the human world justice depends on human beings and not on God. Psalm 115.16 has summed up this idea very aptly:

'The heavens are YHWH's heavens
but the earth he has given to human beings.'

God's whirlwind clears the air. We can look around us with new eyes; we have begun to see that God does not keep to human programmes (of faith) because he regards them as human programmes, not as divine programmes. With such a programme human beings can make a choice when confronted with chaos and order, good and evil, justice and injustice, and give meaning to their lives. But this choice or meaning does not *a priori* coincide with the way in which God deals with human beings.

Job's Reaction: Job 42.1–6

'Job answered YHWH and said,
I know that you can do everything,
and that no purpose of yours can be thwarted.
(You have said,)
"Who is this that veils my governance without knowledge"'?
Indeed I have spoken without insight,
things too wonderful for me, which I did not understand.'
(You have said,)
"Listen and I shall speak.
I have heard you, and you have informed me."
I had heard of you with my ears,
but now my eyes have seen you.
Therefore I have changed my mind
and turn away from dust and ashes' (42.1–6).

Veiling and unveiling

God's speech takes Job's breath away. Only once does he mumble something to himself and remarks that he has nothing to say. God really continues without interruption. And when Job finally has something to say, it is brief; moreover half of it is a quotation of what God says. Thus right at the beginning of his speech, God says:

'Who is this that darkens my governance
by arguments without knowledge?' (38.2)

and Job repeats:

'Who is this that veils my governance without knowledge'?
(42.3).

God spoke about 'darkening' and Job uses the word 'veil'. As also emerges from the verb 'know', which occurs four times, the rest of Job's reaction is also about the lack of knowledge and insight. In his hymn of praise to wisdom, Job celebrated the great capacity of human beings to uncover things: they could bore mines, dig for metals and find precious stones. However, wisdom escaped their urge for discovery. God's stormy account shows Job his lack of insight into everything. If Job still thought that he could show insight and wisdom in his speeches, now he sees that these are as it were nets which he has spread out in order to catch God and the world. But now he realizes that his words veil rather than unveil. Therefore at the beginning of his argument God too raised the question of this veiling or concealing talk. Job now frankly confirms the insight he has achieved and acknowledges that hitherto he has not understood anything (42.3b). Job recognizes in the 'wonderful works' the wholly other that comes upon him in an alienating way and cannot be translated into something that is his or in him. They show something that cannot be grasped or explained, because it has its origin in a transcendent reality. Now that Job has seen this and his knowledge is reduced to a veiling which conceals, he and his own hymn are stripped bare. The 'human' part of his hymn to wisdom and the picture of human capability and (limited) knowledge on earth can remain valid. But the 'divine' part of this hymn, with a description of God and wisdom, is nothing but the product of human imagination. However stimulating this imagination may be for human beings, it cannot refer to a reliable truth. This puts the concluding verses of Job's hymn to wisdom in a different light. Here Job says:

> 'God says to man,
> "Behold, the fear of the Lord is wisdom;
> and to keep far from evil is understanding"' (28.28).

In his speech from the storm God is not requiring human beings or animals to fear him. Nor does Job, in his reaction to God's speech which brings him insight, himself repeat that human beings must refrain from evil deeds and fear God. Does that then mean that they need not fear God, or that they need not strive to do good? God has shown Job through his impressive account that creation contains a broad scale of possibilities:

creation and chaos, life and death, good and evil, love and violence. Through this Job has discovered that it is up to human beings to make choices. They can strive for a life in which doing good comes first and the emphasis lies on love and reverence for the creation. But human beings can equally opt for criminality, selfishness and the destruction of creation. The limited capacities of human knowledge on the one hand and the great range of possibilities on the other make it possible to choose whether or not to believe in (the existence of) God. However great the power of God as creator is, it is up to human beings to recognize God's presence in creation. Job has recognized that believing has thus become a human activity.

Speaking and listening, hearing and seeing

'(You have said,) "Listen and I shall speak.
I have heard you, and you have informed me"' (42.4).

In Job's reaction there is a second quotation from God's speech, in which God says that he has listened to Job and that Job has informed him. This pericope is constructed in a very subtle way around the words 'speak' and 'listen'. Job begins with speaking (v.1) and implicitly says, 'You said, who speaks' (v.3a). Job answers, 'I spoke' (v.3b), and again refers implicitly to God's speaking: 'You said: I shall speak, now that I have heard you speak' (v.4). This exchange between Job and God is concluded in v.5, when Job speaks for the last time and says:

'I had heard of you with my ears,
but now my eyes have seen you.'

After all this talking and listening Job for the first time comes to see and understand. Talking and listening seem to stand for the fixed talk of the tradition, the friends and Job himself, which can be caught in nets. Although they reflect on God and the world, they form words and images for themselves and impose these as necessary structures or demands on the world and on God. But now that Job has heard God speaking in the storm, he has seen God and his cosmos for the first time. In contrast to listening to the words of the tradition and speaking oneself, seeing is a direct experience. Seeing is the perception or experience of something that comes from outside. By contrast, words come from within and are determined and shaped by one's own thought-patterns. Seeing is the experience of 'the other' which cannot be reduced to oneself and is not dependent on oneself. The prologue had already brought out the difference between the contingent, that which is present here and now and is given shape by human beings, and the transcendent, that which comes from outside human beings and transcends them. In the monologues and dialogues which follow, Job and his friends have always started from the contingent and made links between that and the transcendent. God's whirlwind blew all that over: the ideas, the networks of causal relations that they had laid on reality and then attributed to God, have been blown away. They prove to be not necessary but arbitrary relations; they did not express knowledge but were veils. Job has now 'seen' this for the first time. He has caught a glimpse of God's view, and that brings him to a turning-point in his thinking.

The topicality of the problems

Questions and solutions like Job's are also the subject of discussion in our (post-)modern age. Frans Kellendonk has made some apt comments on these problems in his essay 'Great Words'. It can perhaps clarify our position now and that of Job.

The great words of former times have all proved to be empty words. If we can understand anything at all by the word God, this idea does not rest on an immediate experience but on an experience of human inadequacies. It is the same with eternity – that term must be rooted in our experience of time. Absolute good denies the finitude of the good that we experience here, and absolute beauty the transitory nature of earthly beauty. All these terms are denials, and denials do not occur in nature, only in human consciousness. They spring from the desire to close the gap between consciousness and the world, what the poet Wallace Stevens has called the 'absence in reality'. So people have projected beyond the world of phenomena a higher world in which the division is removed, the wish is made

*the father of the thought and colonizes our earth wih the heaven
of ideas, which has devastating results.*

*But there was a time, say before Plato's influence made itself
felt, when the great words sanctified life rather than destroyed
it, honoured human criteria and did not belittle them; and even
after that their influence has not just been unfavourable. They
have given form and direction to desires, and have created community. I think that it must be possible to reconstruct them in
this sense; indeed I think that this is necessary, because while
perhaps you can abolish these great words, you cannot abolish
the longing by which they have always lived. The 'absence in
reality' remains. The way in which these words denied reality
lay in their absolute character and we must get rid of this by
taking them simply for what they are: expressions of desires,
fabrications which could be healthy but become pernicious as
soon as they begin to lead an absolute existence. The religion of
heaven must become a religion of the earth. Faith is then not
certainty but creation. Meaning is then not discovered but
given. Origin and goal do not stand outside history, but are
phenomena which give shape to history from within. The good
does not exist, either in heaven or here, unless it is supported
by an ongoing series of good actions. The holy is that which is
hallowed and God is enthroned on human hymns.*

Is this a (post-)modern account of what we have in Job? In my
view there are ideas here which agree with the book of Job, but
there is also a great difference. Some related ideas appear, for
example in the following sentences: 'People have projected
beyond the world of phenomena a higher world in which the
division is removed, the wish is made the father of the thought
and colonizes our earth with the heaven of ideas, which has
devastating consequences.' And: 'taking them [ideas] simply for
what they are: expressions of desires, fabrications which could
be healthy but become pernicious as soon as they begin to lead
an absolute existence.' Kellendonk does not mention the word
God, does not acknowledge the existence of God and has opted
to call what exists outside human beings, and is almost as intan-
gible as God, 'reality'. But in one respect the problem remains
the same. Both Kellendonk and the book of Job say that people

try to close the gap between reality and human beings, between heaven and earth, by words and ideas which they then absolutize. Both conclude that this is a bad thing. Kellendonk therefore argues for 'making the religion of heaven a religion of the earth'. In the book of Job God makes another proposal in his speech: the gulf between heaven and earth, or between creator and creatures, cannot be closed, and God moves from the specific role of heaven to that of earth, and from earth to that of heaven. As far as the earth is concerned, the consequences which Kellendonk also draws and describes follow from God's argument. Paraphrasing Kellendonk's words, this means that 'the great words which have been formulated to form images and thoughts are meaningful insofar as they give form and direction to human desires and create community, insofar as they lead to good on earth. There is no good on earth unless it is supported by an ongoing series of good deeds. Only what is hallowed on earth is holy. For human beings God is enthroned on human hymns.' That settles the matter for Kellendonk. But it does not apply to the book of Job, because it is only half the story. Heaven continues to exist alongside earth and God is not dependent on human imagination, on human hymns. According to the book of Job, God cannot be reduced to a product of human imagination. In this sense the Jewish philosopher Levinas is more on Job's wavelength when he talks of God in terms of the 'wholly other'; as the Other who is active outside human beings and cannot be reduced to human beings, who is not dependent on the hallowing of human beings and does not need to be given meaning by them.

The insight that Job has gained is that while there is a master plan of creation, its content is known only to God. He knows the origin and purpose of the world: 'God can do everything, and no purpose of God's can be thwarted' (42.2). Job realizes at the end of the book that he cannot know that plan, far less control it. Thus he lets the transcendent God and contingent human beings stand side by side. He does not reduce God to human standards, far less exalt human beings to divine standards. It has been granted to Job to see this. Readers must see it through Job's eyes and words, presented and perhaps even screened by the pen of the narrators. And even after that readers

have only the same fragile ears and language as the friends and
Job.

Is Job defeated?

Job has finally come to understand. You would expect him to
burst out in shouts of joy. But many biblical translations render
what he says, despite the differences between them, as though
he had been defeated:

> 'Therefore I despise myself and repent in dust and ashes'
> (NIV, RSV).
> 'Therefore I yield, repenting in dust and ashes' (REB).

There is no rejoicing here; sorrow dominates. These translations
begin from Job's negative evaluation of his insights in 42.5: 'I
had heard of you with my ears, but now my eyes have seen you.'
Despite the positive insights into the limited nature of his knowledge, Job is said finally to climb down. He surrenders himself
to dust and ashes. However, this strange but very usual interpretation of the book takes no account of the order in the text,
nor of the word 'therefore' at the beginning of Job's conclusion.
Because he has now seen everything clearly at last, does he hang
his head and give up? Inspired by a study made by the Old
Testament scholar Piet de Boer, I want to ask whether this is
indeed the content of 42.6. A somewhat technical examination
is necessary, but it is worth the trouble.

The first verb, *ma'as* in Hebrew, is usually translated 'despise'
in the English translations. This word occurs often in Job, three
times in the first person singular, in 9.21: 'I turn away from my
life'; in 31.13: 'If I turn away from the right of my slave' and
here too in 42.6. So the word *ma'as* means turn away from
something old (negative) and turn towards something new.
Now most translations have exclusively opted for the first
aspect: Job despises his old behaviour. Without wanting to deny
this aspect, one cannot totally omit the second aspect of *ma'as*,
namely conversion or turning towards new behaviour. Turning
away or casting off and turning to belong indissolubly together.
So Job is saying, 'I am turning away from and to . . .'

The second verb, in Hebrew *nacham*, is translated 'repent'.

This verb occurs very often in the Hebrew Bible and has two opposed meanings: 'change', and then often in the sense of be sorry for or take vengeance on, and 'not change', or be at rest in the sense of comfort and reassure. So you could translate here either 'I convert and change' or 'I convert and do not change'. A second aspect of *nacham* which De Boer has pointed out is that *nacham* is followed by *al*, over. The combination *nacham al* occurs seventeen times in the Hebrew Bible and always means 'overlook'. Fourteen times God is the subject of *nacham al*: God overlooks from a disaster, a punishment or prosperity. When human beings are the subject of the verb *nacham al* it is often in connection with the end of a period of mourning and can then be translated 'cease mourning'. Thus the end of David's period of mourning after the death of his son is denoted by *nacham al*: David ceases his mourning, and does not continue to repent over the death of his son. In another text Rachel refuses to stop mourning the loss of her sons, and this is indicated with *nacham al* and a negative. Job 42.6 also belongs in this series. Job gives up his 'dust and ashes' and thus ends the period of mourning.

This leads to the conclusion that the two verbs *ma'as* and *nacham* in 42.6 indicate the change which takes place in Job. Job turns away from the past, gives up his mourning and turns to the future. That does not mean that Job denies his past, but only that he accepts what he has heard and seen and opens himself to new possibilities. Given the order of the text, this is a much more consistent interpretation, and moreover it does justice to the word 'therefore'. God has spoken and shown Job everything and Job reacts: 'I have now seen and therefore I can stop mourning.' Because he has seen, he rediscovers strength and energy to climb up out of the deep valley in which he was sitting. In short, the translation of these verses is:

> 'I had heard of you with my ears,
> but now my eyes have seen you.
> Therefore I have changed my mind,
> and turn away from dust and ashes' (42.5–6).

Chinam *revisited?*

In the prologue of the book of Job the central question is whether human beings believe in God in a disinterested (*chinam*) way. In heaven, the satan and God discuss this question and devise an experiment to investigate whether there is such a thing as disinterested faith. A particularly pious man, Job, is to serve as the test-case. The question is whether this Job believes in God in a disinterested way or only because he is prosperous. Job's faith will only be truly disinterested when he continues to believe without a direct reason and without a special purpose. The satan afflicts Job with setbacks, but even after these harsh blows Job continues as a believer who does not curse God but blesses him. Job emerges from the experiment in the first instance as a pious man, but that is immediately relativized by a demonstration that he finds it natural to think from God's perspective. Here the tradition of faith offers him the means of expressing that perspective, among other things in generally recognized formulae of faith. This emerges from his behaviour towards his children and his reaction to his afflictions: 'The Lord has given and the Lord has taken away; blessed be the name of the Lord.' In chapter 2 of the prologue, when Job is smitten with sickness and what his wife says confronts him with his own death, the doubt increases. His perspective changes. Now he no longer thinks from God's perspective but from a human perspective, in asking 'If we receive good from God, must we not then also receive evil?'. Job goes one step further in chapter 3, his first monologue. He no longer speaks from a general human perspective, but purely from his own perspective. And he no longer knows how to combine his own experiences with the traditional faith that he had confessed hitherto. He continues to believe, but his faith is full of doubt and despair. In the conversations with his friends which follow he sets his own personal experiences over against the traditional conceptions of God and the world. In retrospect one could say that the moment he begins to replace his general piety, expressed in traditional words, in which he was so to speak thinking in the name of God, with thinking and living from his own experience, he makes his own development possible and sets it in motion. This development is characterized by conflict. The dialogue with the friends shows that this is a painful business.

After God's impressive argument, Job sees where he has gone wrong. Previously, in accordance with the tradition in which he and his friends stood, he had created an image of God, spread a network of great words about creation and called for retributive action on God's part. He had thought that in this way he could have a grasp of creation. But the opposite proves to be the case. His network functions only as a smoke-screen. When God's speech removes the concealing mist, Job can see clearly around him, and at that moment he changes, he is converted. Then he changes from being a believer who asks a lot to being a believer who asks for nothing, a *chinam* or disinterested believer.

Now the special attention that we paid to the verb *nacham*, which along with *ma'as* indicates Job's change or conversion, proves to make sense. In the Hebrew this word consists of three letters, *n.ch.m* (Hebrew was originally written only in consonants; the vowels were added later). Job's conversion is thus indicated by the word *nacham*, which is clearly a reversal of the letters *ch.n.m* that make up *chinam*.

Job was first	not a *ch.n.m* believer
Job changes	*n.ch.m*
and becomes	a *ch.n.m* believer

I think that this is the briefest possible summary of the book of Job, a book about a man in the process of growth. It indicates the process of development that Job undergoes, from being a believer who feels that he can think from God's perspective to becoming a believer who sees that God cannot be reduced to the views that human beings have of him. But at the same time he, and the readers with him, see at the end of the book the complete meaning of this *chinam*. *chinam* faith means not only a faith in God without a direct cause or reason and without a purpose or goal, but also a faith which is not necessary but possible. Job now sees that faith is not a divine demand but a human choice. From God's speech Job has come to realize that he cannot gain any essential insight into the ordering of the universe, that knowledge is always the forming of pictures by human beings, and thus also veils. He sees that even believing is a human activity. Human beings try to direct their lives in accordance with a particular programme of faith, so that they have guidelines which help them to create community or hallow the creation and the creator. But they cannot ask anything from God on this basis: they establish possible relations, not necessary relations which also apply to God. Only when Job sees all this can the experiment carried out by God and the satan be said to be a success. After his conversion, Job has finally come through the test brilliantly.

Rudely confronted with another way of looking at things, Job has undergone a change. But this change to real *chinam* believing at the same time means that the final outcome of the story of Job which follows does not say anything about Job's faith, since in *chinam* believing what follows or what has gone before is a matter of indifference. It makes no difference to Job's faith whether subsequently things go well with him in a material or physical respect. Of course it does have an effect on Job as a person, but not on the content of what faith is or needs to be: detached from cause or consequence, a possible choice which offers no guarantee of a good future, far less of a bad future.

Ambiguity in the book of Job

From the beginning of the book I have pointed out how a network of images has been woven into the book of Job. These images are often ambiguous, and are used by different figures in different, sometimes even contradictory, ways. This network can convince the reader that simplicity is hardly possible and that ambiguity is a fact of existence. The multiplicity of images in the book of Job then proves to correspond to its content. Human beings who are confronted with a creation which comprises order and chaos and offers a great many possible meanings are also offered the possibility of making what they will of their lives on earth. They can believe in God; they can strive for a good life or a bad life. They can accuse God of arbitrariness in a world which is full of arbitrary pictures of human beings. But the intention of the book of Job cannot be denied: it is a plea for a view which is not simple, which leaves both human beings and God necessarily free.

The readers of the book of Job are compelled to a similar ambivalent interpretation by its many ambivalent words and images. They are prompted to allow the many different lines of the book of Job to function in their interpretation. For example the words *nacham* and *chinam*, but also the word 'hedge around', put them in a position to see the web that the text has woven and put over the world as a network. The network of the text shows us readers the possibility of giving meaning to our world on the basis of the text and forming pictures of our lives and of God. But our pictures, too, should simultaneously unveil and veil and similarly be a reflection of the many-sidedness of creation and chaos. So we too can never require absoluteness of our pictures of God and the world. Perhaps, like Job, we should be able to undergo a change and suddenly begin to see through other eyes, although real conversions tend to come about through our own experience rather than through reading words.

God's Reaction: Job 42.7–9

'After YHWH had spoken these words to Job,
YHWH said to Eliphaz the Temanite:
"My wrath is kindled against you and your two friends,
for you have not spoken rightly of me,
as my servant Job has.
Now therefore take seven bulls and seven rams,
go to my servant Job,
offer a sacrifice for yourselves,
and have my servant Job pray for you.
I shall lift up his face,
and because of him not do anything evil to you,
for you have not spoken rightly of me,
as my servant Job has."
So Eliphaz the Temanite, Bildad the Shuhite and Zophar the
Naamathite
went and did what YHWH had told them
and YHWH lifted up Job's face.'

Reaction to reaction

God's reaction immediately follows that of Job and relates
to both Job and his friends. Chapter 42 of the book of Job is
usually called the epilogue, but it contains Job's reaction
(42.1–6), God's reaction (42.7–9) and the narrator's reaction
(42.10–17) to what has gone before, one after the other.
Together these reactions form the last scene in the play, which
rounds it off: all the actors appear once again, as the play is
nearly over. Job and God appear once again; only the role of the
satan is played out. That is because Job has converted or, better,
has grown into a real *chinam* believer. The friends have not
grown into heroes, but they are allowed on stage once again,

not, as is usual in a normal play, to receive applause but to get told off.

This closing chapter is largely constructed in parallel to the prologue (Job 1–2). Thus the question of *chinam* is central in Job's reaction in 42.1–6, as it is in the first part of the prologue. Moreover in 42.10–17, the very last part of the book, we have a recurrence of the term *barak,* which played such an important role in the prologue. But above all God's reaction in 42.7–9 corresponds closely to the prologue. The way in which the friends are presented in 42.7–9 recalls the introduction of the three friends in the prologue (2.11–13). First of all there is the repetition of their names and the places from which they come: Eliphaz the Temanite, Bildad the Shuhite and Zophar the Naamathite. Then they are still always addressed as 'friend'. It is striking that in the first instance God addresses himself to Eliphaz, the chief of them, 'and his two friends'. In this way God makes it implicitly clear that they prove to be more one another's friends than friends of Job. There is another parallel in the world 'servant'. Neither in the dialogues nor in God's speech is Job called God's servant, but only in the prologue. Four times in two verses God calls Job 'my servant'. Other parallel elements can be mentioned. Just as in the prologue Job mediates for his sons with God by means of (burnt) offerings, so in 42.8 Job has to mediate for his friends with God by means of (burnt) offerings. And last but not least, we are struck by the characteristic contrast between the terms *napal,* fall or prostrate, in the prologue, and *nasa,* raise up, in 42.7–9. In the prologue Sabaeans and Chaldaeans attack, blows and sickness strike Job down, and he falls to the earth. Down but not out, Job emerges from the battle and at the end of the book his face is again raised up by God.

God's rebuke to the friends

The friends who appear on stage once again do not get any thanks for all their help and support to Job, but a telling-off. God twice makes precisely the same criticism of them: 'You have not spoken rightly of me, as my servant Job has'

(42.7, 8). What does he mean by this? Have they really spoken so differently from Job?

The friends are confronted with the facts of Job's extraordinarily great suffering, which does not correspond to their ideas of retributive justice or to their idea of God. They then do not adapt their views to reality but reality to theory. First they still see that Job is pious and that his wretchedness cannot be due to lack of piety. Later their views change, and they begin to regard Job as less pious and perhaps even as a sinner, so that their theory of retribution continues to fit. The difference between Job, who for much of the book also holds on to a belief in retribution, and his friends, is that Job continues to see that his experience of the facts does not correspond to the theory. He continues to look for a way of making the two match, without sacrificing the facts to the theory. He doesn't give up. He makes progress not only through his combativeness but above all through his capacity to recognize that experience and traditional theology cannot be reconciled. Here his belief in God is the motive force behind his incessant struggle. Some people use God as a stop-gap or as a means of sorting everything out. With Job it is precisely the reverse. His faith in God does not defeat him, does not lead him to a cowardly tranquillity, but forces him to keep going. He uses his faith in God as a battering ram to break things open. Precisely because he cannot understand how a God who is just in human eyes can allow suffering, he feels compelled to look further than the theory which has been handed down to him and which he too still confesses passionately. But Job has experienced in person the clash between facts and theory, and has to recognize the lack of agreement between the two. For that reason Job can grow and the friends cannot. Job gradually recognizes the fault in his framework of thought and faith, and learns from the fault. The friends continue to think that their framework of thought is the only possible and only good one. Therefore the book of Job is ultimately an optimistic book, because it shows that there is hope for growth as long as clashes with experienced reality are noted, as they are by Job, and not disguised or smoothed over.

Finally, it is very important to read God's reprimand to the friends at the place where it stands in the book, namely in

42.7–9 and after Job's reaction in 42.1–6. Only when Job has let himself be blown over, begins to see the new constellation, and repents, does God react to him and praise him as his good servant. Only when it proves that the friends, having heard the same speech by God, do not say 'We have heard God and seen that we got things wrong. Therefore we are converted,' does God react to the friends and rebuke them. It is not that the narrator gives the friends no opportunity to say this. By their attitude before God's speech the friends had already shown that they were incapable of looking honestly at the facts and their own false interpretation of them. They were still not ready to recognize that something in their system did not add up. Unlike Job, they were not in a position to change their view and attitude under the influence of God's speech.

Like the friends, Job tries to close the gap between earth and heaven with a network of ideas. Unlike the friends, Job realizes that his network does not fit, precisely because he continues to do justice to his experience of the world. This combination puts Job in a position to grow in the way which he has experienced. It is only as both a servant of God and as a realist who is ready to let himself be blown over by the storm that Job is valued more by God than the friends. God endorses his evaluation with 'my servant Job', repeated four times. In reaction to the change in Job God himself now changes: the one who had had Job smitten down now raises him up; the one who felled Job now lifts up his face.

The book could have ended there. Job and God have changed. However, the narrator felt the need to make the change complete and at the end of the book to have a complete restoration of the prosperous situation in which Job found himself at the beginning of the prologue.

The Narrator's Reaction:
Job 42.10–17

10 And YHWH restored the fortunes of Job, when he had prayed for his friends; and YHWH doubled Job's possessions 11. All his brothers and sisters and all who had known him before came to him and ate bread with him in his house. And they showed him compassion and comforted him for all the evil that YHWH had brought upon him. And each of them gave him a piece of silver and a ring of gold. 12. And YHWH blessed the latter days of Job more than the former days. He had fourteen thousand sheep, six thousand camels, a thousand yoke of oxen, and a thousand she-asses.

13. He also had seven sons and three daughters. 14. He called the first Jemimah, the second Keziah and third Keren-happuch. 15. In all the land there were no women so fair as Job's daughters; and their father gave them an inheritance among their brothers. 16. After this Job lived a hundred and forty years, and saw his children and his grandchildren to the fourth generation. 17. So Job died, an old man, and full of days.

Mrs Job again

How amazed we are when Job suddenly still seems to have brothers and sisters! We are even more amazed when without any mention of his wife, Job gets another ten children. Poor Mrs Job! She is not consoled; the brothers and sisters come to see her husband, not to see her. Once, right at the beginning of the book, she has been allowed to say something, but that was all. At that time she suggested that her spouse should say *barak* to God, i.e. bless and/or say good-bye to God, and confronted him with his death. She also set Job thinking at that time. But however meaningful her remark might have been for Job's development and for the book written about him, things turned out worse for her. Since then her role has ended and she has been written out of the play, although now, at the end of the book, she is ten times put in the state of *barak* and thus also contributes her bit to her husband's happiness.

The word *barak* also has a role in this pericope in a different way. Verse 42.12 reads: 'YHWH blessed (*barak*) the latter days of Job more than the former days.' Only then does it become evident that there are two trajectories along which *barak* can take place, namely God's trajectory and the human trajectory. The blessing of human beings by God in the form of a prosperous life seems independent of the blessing of God by human beings. Thus for example God does not bless God at a time when Job blesses him (1.21), and Job no longer blesses God when things go very badly with him. There is thus no causal connection between these two trajectories. God blesses when it suits him, and Job and other human being bless when it suits them. To put it in a more friendly way, believing *chinam* is one side of this coin and God's blessing is the other, equally free, side of the same coin. At the end of the book Job does not know the cause of his trials, far less the reason for his restoration. Both are a total surprise to him: God's blessing or lack of blessing also comes upon human beings *chinam*: it is given without necessity or purpose.

The narrator does not put any emphasis on Mrs Job. Her role at the beginning of the book was important but not extensive. Later in the book Job himself presents a limited picture of a wife, conditioned by its context: the wife is important only in relation to her husband. The narrator seems to see things in the same way. That can make it clear to the present-day reader that the images which the narrator uses are also conditioned by their place and time.

Job's daughters

Job has a new family: ten new children are born to him. In contrast to the prologue, to which his feasting sons were central, now all Job's interest is in his attractive daughters with long, incomprehensible names. Not only does Job find his daughters attractive, but each of them also gets a dowry. What role do these daughters play here? The writer could have wanted to indicate that Job was so crazy about his daughters that he gave them a dowry, contrary to the rules of the time. That would then be a proof of Job's love. Another possibility is that Job is so rich that he could give a dowry to the three daughters without his sons suffering as a result. In that case this part of the text would be an indication of Job's wealth.

However, I think that the function of the daughters in this epilogue is primarily different. The prologue describes the sons and their behaviour, to which Job reacted with religious obligations and scrupulous piety. This epilogue describes his daughters and their physical beauty, and Job reacts with enjoyment: he is happy with his daughters and gives them attractive names. He is no longer the scrupulous and formal pious man who has to keep everything under control. He enjoys things more than ever before.

The conclusion of the book of Job

The narrator describes how well things are with Job: they are very good, possibly even better than before. Job has just as many children and far more cattle than he had. His burdensome wife is not mentioned again. The reader can read this idyllic description, this happy ending in 42.10–17, in three totally different ways.

The first and most usual reaction is one of deep disappointment. The narrator hasn't understood anything of the whole book of Job. For such a happy ending undermines his own book. All the old principle of retribution is reinstated. What a disappointment, a real blow!

Another possibility is that the narrator or redactor has indeed understood the opposition to retribution in the book but wanted to make it acceptable for the canon of the Hebrew Bible by including this last part. The principle of retribution is in fact often central to these other books of the Bible. The Torah or Pentateuch, the first five books, give a basic law or programme of faith for human beings. If they follow that programme, they and their children will be rewarded by God. If they do not follow that programme and do not live in accordance with the precepts of the Torah, then they and their children will be punished by God to the umpteenth generation. What is this, if not a working out of the principle of retribution? Now since these texts are holy and have been included in the list of holy books or the canon, if the book of Job is also to be included, the discussion about this principle of retribution in Job and especially the outcome must be toned down. Otherwise Job's image of God would begin to differ too much from that in the rest of the Hebrew Bible. The last pericope then tones down, if not undermines, the whole book, with the aim of keeping the book of Job in the canon of the Hebrew Bible.

However, it is also possible to read the conclusion in a totally different way, which implies that the narrator has both understood the book well and has written this conclusion in line with the rest of the book. The conclusion in 42.10–17 then does not undermine the rest of the book of Job but reinforces it. Readers are then wrong in objecting to the ultimately good outcome of the book of Job. These readers would have liked the principle of retribution to be abandoned, and therefore would have liked no reward or punishment to follow at the end. But in that case they have forgotten that if believing is really *chinam*, both a bad and a good situation can be possibilities, not as a reward of Job's behaviour but as God's free action. In that case the end no longer has anything to do with what it follows. Whether Job remains poor or becomes rich does not say anything about his disinterested faith. Perhaps one could put this even more clearly. The narrator may have hoped to hold his readers' attention more and to compel them to reflect on the consequences of *chinam* belief by opting for a good outcome rather than for a bad one. Had he opted for a bad outcome, then people could have concluded that just as previously retribution was *the* paradigm or framework of thought, so from now on non-retribution had become *the* paradigm. In that case one certain system would have replaced another certain system. But the opposite is the case, since the book of Job has wanted to show quite specifically that simplicity has been replaced by ambiguity. Perhaps retribution no longer holds, but if people were now to opt for sheer injustice, precisely the same logic would follow.

Perhaps readers do most justice to the book of Job if they recognize the three ways of reading the narrator's reaction. The first two begin from the fact that the writer has composed a book that is 'finished', both according to the laws of narrative art and according to the norms of the canon. The third reading, which is at the same time present and is possibly even stronger, is that the author has given the book of Job an ending in which the readers can see precisely what *chinam* belief involves: a faith with which you cannot compel anything, and with which you cannot explain or predict the future, far less demand justice from God. In that case the book of Job is a book which is not finished, since down to the present day readers continue to puzzle over it and occupy themselves intensively with it. And precisely that could be one of the aims of the author.

Bibliography

Sources

'De vos in de wijnberg', *Joodse Sprookjes*, Elmar, Rijswijk 1990, 176
'Verwelkte bladeren', *Joodse Sprookjes*, Elmar, Rijswijk 1990, 97
Nooteboom, C., 'Scholastiek', *vuurtijd, ijstijd, Gedichten 1955–1983*, Arbeiderspers, Amsterdam 1984
Versnel, H.S., 'Geloof het of niet', *Trouw*, December 1990
Linden, N. ter, 'Het verhaal van de herdersjongen', in Grootmoeder vertelt, *Trouw*, July 1990
Kellendonk, F., 'Naschrift: Grote Woorden', *Geschilderd eten*, Nijhoff/Meulenhoff, Amsterdam 1988, 74–83

General literature on Job

Biblia Hebraica Stuttgartensia, Job (ed. G.Gerleman), Württembergische Bibelanstalt, Stuttgart 1974
Tanakh–the Holy Scripture, Job, The New Jewish Publication Society Translation According to the Traditional Hebrew Text, Philadelphia, New York and Jerusalem 1988
Alter, R., 'Truth and Poetry in the Book of Job', in *The Art of Biblical Narrative*, Basic Books, New York 1985, 85–110
Boer, P. A. H. de, 'Does Job retract?', in *Selected Studies in Old Testament Exegesis*, ed. C.van Duin, Brill, Leiden 1991, 179–95
Brenner, A., 'Job the Pious? The Characterization of Job in the Narrative Framework of the Book', *Journal for the Study of the Old Testament* 43, 1989, 37–52
Cheney, M.S., *Piety and Parody in the Book of Job* (in preparation)
Clines, D.J.A., *Job 1–20*, Word Biblical Commentary 17, Word Books, Dallas 1989
—, 'Deconstructing the Book of Job', in *What does Eve do to help?*, Journal for the Study of the Old Testament Supplement Series, Sheffield 1990, 106–23
Cox, D., 'A Rational Inquiry into God: Chapters 4–27 of the Book of Job', *Gregorianum* 67, 1986, 621–58

Fohrer, G., *Das Buch Hiob*, Kommentar zum Alten Testament, Gerd Mohn, Gütersloh 1963

Gordis, R., *The Book of Job. Commentary, New Translation and Special Studies,* Moreshet Series II, The Jewish Theological Seminary of America, New York 1978

Greenberg. M., 'Job', in *The Literary Guide to the Bible*, ed. R.Alter and F. Kermode, The Belknap Press of Harvard University Press, Cambridge, Mass. 1987, 283–304

Habel, N.C., *The Book of Job. A Commentary*, Old Testament Library, SCM Press, London and Westminster Press, Philadelphia 1985

Horst, F., *Hiob*, Biblischer Kommentar. Altes Testament XVl/I, Neukirchener Verlag, Neukirchen 1962

Pope, M. H., *Job. Introduction, Translation and Notes*, Anchor Bible 15, Doubleday, Garden City 1965

Nelis, J.T., *Job*, Boeken van het Oude Testament, Romen, Roermond 1968

Tsevat, M., *The Meaning of the Book of Job and other Biblical Studies. Essays on the Literature and Religion of the Hebrew Bible,* Ktav, New York 1980, 1–37

Vogels. W., *Job*, Belichting van het bijbelboek, Katholieke Bijbelstichting, Boxtel 1989